Unity

Chiara Lubich

Unity

Edited by
Donato Falmi and Florence Gillet

NEW CITY PRESS
of the Focolare
Hyde Park, NY

Published in the United States by New City Press
202 Comforter Blvd., Hyde Park, NY 12538
www.newcitypress.com
©2015 New City Press (English Translation)
Translated by Carlos Bajo from the original Italian
L'Unita, by Chiara Lubich, edited by Donato Falmi e Florence
Gillet
©2015 Città Nuova Editrice, Rome, Italy

Cover design by Leandro De Leon and Durva Correia

Library of Congress Control Number 2015950767

ISBN 978–1–56548–593–8

Printed in the United States of America

Presentation of the book series[*]

"To those who follow you, leave only the gospel."

Chiara Lubich has articulated the gospel in many ways, which are outlined in twelve cornerstones: *God-love*, the *will of God*, the *Word of God*, *love of neighbor*, the *new commandment*, the *Eucharist*, the gift of *unity, Jesus crucified and forsaken, Mary,* the *Church-communion,* the *Holy Spirit, Jesus present among us.*

Since they emerged in the late 1940s, these points have been inscribed in the souls and in the lives of thousands of people from every corner of the earth. Nevertheless, since Chiara Lubich's death in 2008, what has been missing is a document that combined many texts, including those yet unpublished, that would illustrate them. This series of books seeks to deepen our understanding of these twelve cornerstones by presenting three sources from which they have emerged:

- the dimension of her personal testimony, especially as Chiara Lubich understood, deepened and lived these points;

- the theological dimension of reflecting on the mystery of God and of humankind;

---

[*]   This volume contains Chiara Lubich's thought and experience on "unity." While it is the seventh in this series of titles originally published in Italian by Città Nuova, it is the first to be translated in its complete form and published by New City Press. Other volumes in the series will be translated and published.

- the dimension of incarnating these points in human life via a communitarian experience, in line with Vatican II (see Lumen Gentium 9).

The series will include as many as twelve books, through which it is hoped that readers may discover:

- A great spiritual teacher who can accompany them in their spiritual life;

- A deeper appreciation of the communal aspect of Christian life, and the implications of a communitarian spirituality for the Church and humanity;

- A deeper and more personal understanding of Chiara Lubich's life and thought that they can apply in their everyday life.

Contents

Presentation of the book series v

Introduction 1

  Unity: an interweaving of theological, ascetical and
    mystical dimensions 2
  The metaphor of a long and mighty river 3
  The source — Gospel of John Chapter 17 5
  The flow of the river grows 7

A discourse that only the Father
  fully understood 11

  The Prayer of Jesus in John 17:1–26 13

Chapter 1

The Gift of a Charism 17

1. Reading John 17 —
  "An Event of Great Importance" 17
  The story in the writings of the early times 18
  Unity, basis of our every action 23
  To Carry Out the Testament of Jesus 24
  Jesus Crucified as the model 26
  The root of the gift 26
2. A Lifetime Project 28
  Charisms 28
  Keep one idea fixed in your head: unity 30
  What if unity were pronounced by the Almighty? . 30
  Unity and nothing else 32

What characterizes us? 33
Our only goal: to be consumed in one 33
Our rock: Unity 34
What does God want from us? 37

Chapter 2

Unity is Unity with God and the Design of God on History 39

1. Unity in One Word: It's a Person 39
   Unity: wonder and gift 40
   Above all, be one 43
   Unity shows the Risen Lord to the world 44
   Unity, Jesus among us, is the fullness of joy 45
2. Unity is First of All, Unity with God 45
   Jesus: our model 46
   To be, and then to speak and act 47
   Only two Saints can Form a Perfect Unity 48
   Only God with God can achieve unity 50
   Unity and the Eucharist 51
3. Unity is Unity in God Trinity 52
   The Unity which is not founded on Jesus
   is a utopia 52
   The Word of God lived out causes unity 54
   Doing the will of God brings about unity 55
4. Unity is a Grace That Comes from Above .. 56
   Only Jesus among us can fulfill his Testament 56
   A grace that comes from above 57
5. Unity is God's Design on History 58
   The prayer of Jesus for unity is universal 58
   Unity is the summary of Revelation 59
   Unity is God's design for humanity 59

Chapter 3

Unity in Paradise '49, a prophetic and founding experience

Unity in Paradise '49, a prophetic and founding experience 61

The pact with Igino Giordani 62
We will only be Word of God 66
Unity and disunity in the afterlife 67
Love, unity and Trinity 67
Ascetics and mystics 69
The way of Unity 72
Prayer in community 75
The mystical rose 76
To be another Jesus 77

Chapter 4

How to contribute to unity

How to contribute to unity 79

A personal, constant and radical commitment 79
1. Believe, Pray, Contemplate 80
Believing in Jesus present in unity 80
Trust in the prayer of Jesus to the Father 82
To see in each person a candidate for unity 82
Pray 84
Contemplate the life of the Trinity 85
2. Love 87
Service 87
Keeping alive the current of love and peace 88
Knowing how to lose, how to give in 89
Mercy and forgiveness 91
3. Becoming What We Are 92
It is Christ who lives in me 94
Being fulfilled in unity 96

4. The Secret of Unity 99
   The door that opens unity 99
   To love Jesus Forsaken in the difficulties 101
   Unity is only a vague dream without
     love for Jesus forsaken 101
   Love the suffering caused by every disunity 103
5. How to Contribute to the Unity of the
   Churches 105
   Spreading love and reciprocal love among the
     Churches 105
   With the dialogue of life, a "Christian people"
     is composed 107
   A prayer for unity among Churches 109

Chapter 5

Universal brotherhood and a united world 113

   What is our vocation: Unity or universal brother-
     hood? 115
   Understanding and spreading the spirit
     of brotherhood 116
   For the "gestation of a new world" 118
   Living for a united world 121
   Do not be afraid to speak of unity 123
   Spread a powerful current of brotherhood 126
   Unity: the medicine for today's world 127
   Unity and universality 130

Chapter 6

The "rainbow" as expression
of the life of unity 133

Initial intuitions 134
1. The "Colors" – the Life of Unity
   Considered from Different,
   Interconnected Perspectives 135
2. A look at the individual colors 140
   Communion of goods (red) 140
   Witness and outreach (orange) 142
   Spirituality and prayer life (yellow) 143
   Nature and the physical life (green) 146
   Harmony and surroundings (blue) 149
   Wisdom and study (indigo) 151
   Unity and the means of communication (violet) . 154
   The fable that blossomed along Foco Lane 156

Conclusion 159

A heart full of human-divine love 160
The "I desire" of love 161

Endnotes 163

About Chiara Lubich 169

About the editors .... see inside back cover

Introduction

This volume contains Chiara Lubich's thought and experience on "unity." It is the seventh in this series, each of which explores one of the twelve cornerstones of the gospel-based spirituality, each of them one facet of the charism that she received.

Two particular characteristics distinguish unity from other points of the spirituality. First, for many, the word unity does not necessarily have a religious or Christian connotation. In fact, it is closely linked to human realities that we express through words such as friendship, love, or reconciliation. It evokes harmony, peace with oneself and with others. For nations or groups, unity can be synonymous with life, progress, strength. It is therefore a longing, a profound desire in the human heart. On the other hand, in the course of history, the word unity has also taken on controversial meanings of struggle or opposition, of "unity against" and not "for," for individuals as well as for nations. It then transforms itself into totalitarianism, homogenization and coercive uniformity, into domination of some over others. In fact, during the 1940s, even while Chiara discovered it and elaborated it, in the name of unity others oppressed entire nations. Providentially, however, the history of the word unity is not limited to such negative political realities.

Unity is also a key word in contemporary Christianity, which after centuries of struggle, has rediscovered the yearning to return to a time when we were "one heart and one mind," brothers and sisters in Christ, not rivals and enemies. It is the ecumenical aspiration to which the Holy Spirit is urging Christian Churches and ecclesial communities. This aspiration is shared, unequivocally, also by the Catholic Church, which in the Second Vatican Council, defined itself as "a sacrament or as a sign and instrument both of a very closely knit union with God and of the unity of the whole human race."* The Catholic Church seeks unceasingly to build unity. "Our world needs unity, this is an age in which all need unity," said Pope Francis.[1]

The second attribute of this cornerstone of the charism linked to Chiara's experience and thought is that it "names" her *whole* spirituality; indeed, it is called "the spirituality of unity." One of her statements expresses this clearly: in the context of the other eleven cornerstones, unity "expresses, even by itself, what the Spirit wants from us."[2] By itself! This indicates its richness of meaning, its relevance and its complexity. Hence the need to "unfold it" in order to offer an "interpretive key" to the entire gospel.

Unity: an interweaving of theological, ascetical and mystical dimensions

For more than sixty years, Chiara spoke of unity as a light whose content was gradually

---

* See Lumen Gentium 1.

deepened and enriched with new elements, while being communicated to, and experienced by, a growing number of people. In Chiara's thought and experience the word unity does not have just one meaning; it contains a rich tapestry of layers which articulate it in its various theological, ascetic and mystical dimensions, with fruitful social applications.

The metaphor of a long and mighty river

The interweaving of these layers suggests the image of a long and mighty river. "Unity" in the thought and the life of Chiara has, metaphorically, a source, tributaries, branches (which flow away from the main stream), and an access to the sea. This metaphor can be understood along the lines of the prophecy that we find in Ezekiel chapter 47. In Ezekiel, the river flowing from the temple grows rapidly, sprouting trees on its banks, its waters teeming with large numbers of fish. The river flows into the sea, giving it new and fresh water. The same is true of unity, which like every river, flows from a source: for Chiara it is chapter 17 of the Gospel of John. This abundant water is enriched by the contribution of many tributaries which strengthen its flow: other passages of the gospel, (in fact the entire New Testament can be read as the source of unity);* the Magisterium

---

* "[After] having penetrated [the Testament of Jesus] - as God wanted it and as far as God wanted—it was easier to understand the rest of the Gospel. Often we use this example: imagine a plain, this plain is the whole Gospel and deep down [that is, under] the plain lies the Testament

of the Catholic Church; and the Second Vatican Council. Remarkably, the understanding and the experience of unity has been enriched by the increasingly frequent, familial contacts with lay people and influential personalities of the various Christian Churches, who have created a particular type of ecumenism, an ecumenism of life. Moreover, the other aspects or pillars of the spirituality have enriched our understanding of unity, in particular the Word of God, the Eucharist, Jesus forsaken, the presence of Jesus in the midst of the community. And like a river, unity has spread its waters through various branches: universal brotherhood, the desire for a "united world," the dialogue with faithful of non-Christian religions and with people of no religious affiliation. And the flow into the ocean symbolizes the injection of life and benefits that unity lived out gives to humanity, as the river mentioned by Ezekiel

---

of Jesus, which is the summary of the Gospel. Jesus, after having come among us, taught us unity, the very subject of the Testament of Jesus; He made us penetrate unity, we entered unity. Having entered unity, going deep down into it, we understood the roots of all the other Words, so we understood the rest of the Gospel, because we penetrated it through its summary. It was like the ground was pierced to make us penetrate and understand the rest of the Gospel from the inside, understanding it at the root, in its deepest sense." Chiara Lubich, *La Parola di Dio*, Florence Gillet, ed. (Rome: Città Nuova, 2011), 27.

The thought and the experience of Chiara Lubich also contains reference to the thought of St. Paul because she affirms that her Ideal is "living according to the Mystical Body" (see Rm 12:4ff), which for her is the highest expression of Christian life. She also refers frequently to the Eucharist, the bond of unity (see 1 Cor 10:16–17).

heals the waters. And here the metaphor widens, because that river is full of fish and wherever it flows, everything lives. A single river from a single source—unity—but also a multiplicity of places that are watered, nourished, preserved.

The source — Gospel of John Chapter 17

We look now in detail at the spring that provides water to the entire river. Chapter 17 of John was the "founding" text, the "event" from which the gift of unity flowed to Chiara. In the 1940s she is said to have read it and explained it all at once, from beginning to end, to her companions. For Chiara those words were "radiant." That chapter, which is "difficult to understand," certainly gives us an initial interpretation of unity.

We provide the reader with a quick mention of it. The chapter, the pinnacle of the fourth Gospel, opens a window on the relationship between the Father and the Son, fully revealing the communion between them. The entire prayer is set in a particular "place," that of the communion between the two Divine Persons. Thus, what comes to the fore first is the relationship of the Son with the Father, the unity of God. Second, the unity of humankind with God and, finally, that of human beings with each other.

The main object of the prayer is the Son's solicitude regarding the disciples that he had received from the Father, in order to make them enter with him into the Trinitarian communion. The Son prays, "Holy Father, protect them in your name" (Jn 17:11) because as scripture scholars explain — "his holy name" is like a *temple*, a reserved place where Jesus asks that believers "be protected."[3]

All of Chiara's texts are permeated by this Trinitarian dimension, by the relationship of the Father and the Son in the Spirit. Chiara intends unity as the will of Jesus to "bring everyone into the comm-Unity of the Three."

A recurring theme in the passages where Chiara speaks of unity is that of "being another Jesus," an expression not found in John 17, but that somehow conveys the profound intention of Jesus contained in such words, which is to be assimilated to Him,* to make us sons and daughters in Him-Son.

Another theme related to the source is that the unity of God is the model of the unity of the disciples: "We looked at the unity of the heavenly Father with the divine Son." That unity is also the source, because authentic unity is "Trinitarian life [that] flows freely in us." The commentators on John 17 emphasize that unity among believers has value only if it originates and is rooted in God, in that "We" formed by the communion of the divine Persons.

Furthermore, this anthology also refers to the vital and inseparable connection between unity and Jesus crucified and forsaken. He is the giver of unity, the way, the key to reach unity. This is not expressly stated in John 17, but the theme

---

*   This intention is inferred from the teaching of the entire chapter, particularly in the "I desire" of verse 24: "I desire that those also, whom you have given me, may be with me where I am."

of the glorification and of the glory, which reappears at the beginning of each section, is inextricably tied to the fulfillment of the work that the Father has entrusted to the Son (see Jn 17:4). This fulfillment is necessarily oriented towards the cross, because it is an essential element of the work to be done.

The flow of the river grows

It was natural that unity, both a gift and a life program, would lead to dialogues, to efforts to create or recreate a dialogue. That "all" of John 17 ("that they may all be one") is the engine of Chiara's life and urges her to go toward the divided parts of the church or humanity. This does not occur without the contribution of providential events. And it is in this way that unity becomes dialogue, brotherhood, and united world. But it is also joy, abundant fruits, peace, harmony. Of course, all this has a price—it requires an ascetical, constant, and radical effort. Consequently, there are varied ways of living unity concretely in our life and in our relationships with others.

We have tried to gather the many facets of this prism in the different chapters that comprise this book, bringing one or the other into focus, step by step. The brief introductions are intended to show the common theme that ties them together.

It is logical, therefore, to provide, as a premise, the entire text of chapter 17 of the Gospel of John, which you can use as a reference as you read through this book, to help you discover the main key to the interpretation of the passages from Chiara that we have chosen.

Six chapters follow this premise. The first three regard unity as a gift of God and as an experience of God: the texts we provide help to understand what unity is. The first chapter highlights the light and the joy of this discovery, and the subsequent calling to make the prayer of Jesus resonate to the ends of the world; the second chapter focuses on the essence of unity as the life of God and the life of humankind; the third chapter provides texts that date back to a particular experience, when Chiara lived and understood unity in a prophetic and foundational way during the summer of 1949. It is worth noting how this extraordinary mystical experience is characterized right away as communitarian and collective. The last three chapters deal with the more practical aspects of unity, inasmuch as unity is also a journey for humankind that is expressed in many ways. In particular, we consider the attitudes needed in order to receive the gift of unity (chapter 4); what unity is today in our world, as it blossoms into universal brotherhood and in working for a united world (chapter 5). The concluding chapter offers a model to order our personal and social life according to a style of relationships based on unity.

These texts represent different literary genres, some more concrete, others more mystical, some more educational, others more prophetic; they include passages from diaries, official speeches, or slightly edited talks to her extended spiritual family. First and foremost, they extend an invitation to experience them. In fact, as Jean Guitton writes, "The desire of every author is that his work be fulfilled in a soul,"[4] a statement particularly true of Chiara.

The following pages do not presume, therefore, to provide an external and purely cognitive insight about unity. Instead, they offer an opportunity for an internal and existential understanding, an invitation to let ourselves be drawn into the prayer of Jesus for unity, a prayer that we believe God treasures before, and much more, than we do.

Donato Falmi and Florence Gillet

A discourse that only the Father fully understood

Reading chapter 17 of the Gospel of John at an unknown date in a dark place, — perhaps in a basement[5] — gave rise to the charism of unity. We offer a closer look at this particular gospel passage, introduced by a brief text of Chiara:

If you have the good fortune to be in the Holy Land in the spring, among the thousands of things that Jerusalem offers for contemplation and meditation, one strikes you in a unique way, because of what it calls to mind, in its extreme simplicity. Impervious to time and weathered by two thousand years, a long, stone stairway, punctuated here and there with poppies, reddish like the blood of the Passion, leads down, like a falling rippled ribbon, pristine and solemn, towards the Kidron Valley.

It is still bare, out in the open, skirted by a grassy field, almost as if no vaulted monument could substitute the sky that crowns it. Tradition tells us that Jesus walked down that stairway on his last night, after supper, "looked up to heaven," which was flooded with stars, and said: "Father, the hour has come ..." (Jn 17:1).

It is stirring to put your feet in the same place touched by the feet of God. Your whole soul bursts forth from you as you look up at the same sky that God gazed on. This feeling can be so powerful that your meditation turns into adoration.

His was a unique prayer before dying. And the more this "Son of Man," whom you adore, radiates God, the more you sense his human nature, and you are enamored. His is a discourse that only the Father fully understood; and yet, he voiced it out in the open, perhaps so that an echo of such a beautiful melody could reach us.

December 15, 1959[6]

The Prayer of Jesus in John 17:1–26

1 After Jesus had spoken these words, he looked up to heaven and said, "Father, the hour has come; glorify your Son so that the Son may glorify you,

2 since you have given him authority over all people, to give eternal life to all whom you have given him.

3 And this is eternal life, that they may know you, the only true God, and Jesus Christ whom you have sent.

4 I glorified you on earth by finishing the work that you gave me to do.

5 So now, Father, glorify me in your own presence with the glory that I had in your presence before the world existed.

6 I have made your name known to those whom you gave me from the world. They were yours, and you gave them to me, and they have kept your word.

7 Now they know that everything you have given me is from you;

8 for the words that you gave to me I have given to them, and they have received them and know in truth that I came from you; and they have believed that you sent me.

9 I am asking on their behalf; I am not asking on behalf of the world, but on behalf

of those whom you gave me, because they are yours.

10 All mine are yours, and yours are mine; and I have been glorified in them.

11 And now I am no longer in the world, but they are in the world, and I am coming to you. Holy Father, protect them in your name that you have given me, so that they may be one, as we are one.

12 While I was with them, I protected them in your name that you have given me. I guarded them, and not one of them was lost except the one destined to be lost, so that the scripture might be fulfilled.

13 But now I am coming to you, and I speak these things in the world so that they may have my joy made complete in themselves.

14 I have given them your word, and the world has hated them because they do not belong to the world, just as I do not belong to the world.

15 I am not asking you to take them out of the world, but I ask you to protect them from the evil one.

16 They do not belong to the world, just as I do not belong to the world.

17 Sanctify them in the truth; your word is truth.

18 As you have sent me into the world, so I have sent them into the world.

19 And for their sakes I sanctify myself, so that they also may be sanctified in truth.

20 I ask not only on behalf of these, but also on behalf of those who will believe in me through their word,

21 that they may all be one. As you, Father, are in me and I am in you, may they also be in us, so that the world may believe that you have sent me.

22 The glory that you have given me I have given them, so that they may be one, as we are one,

23 I in them and you in me, that they may become completely one, so that the world may know that you have sent me and have loved them even as you have loved me.

24 Father, I desire that those also, whom you have given me, may be with me where I am, to see my glory, which you have given me because you loved me before the foundation of the world.

25 Righteous Father, the world does not know you, but I know you; and these know that you have sent me.

26 I made your name known to them, and I will make it known, so that the love with which you have loved me may be in them, and I in them."

Chapter 1

The Gift of a Charism

The texts presented in this chapter describe in general terms the source of the gift of unity and how this "discovery" is linked to those that had previously been made (the Word of God, mutual love, the effort to refer constantly to Jesus, especially to Jesus in his Passion and in his abandonment). All is composed in a synthesis of light and wisdom.

1. Reading John 17 — "An Event of Great Importance"

We also remember that one of the first pages of the Gospel which we read — we who were just young women — was the Testament of Jesus (John 17).

It was an event of great importance.

The memory is still vivid in our minds of how, as we moved from one word to the next, each word seemed more illuminated. And now we understand that it was as if someone were telling us: "Look, in the school of Jesus, you have many things to learn, but what sums it all up are the words of his Testament:

> *Sanctify them in the truth ...*
> *that they may all be one ...*
> *You will have the fullness of joy ...*
> *may they also be in us ...*

And we understood it with an awareness that can only be attributed to a special grace, because otherwise it would have been impossible since the Testament of Jesus is the most difficult part of the Gospel.

Rocca di Papa, Italy,
January 25, 1975 [7]

The story in the writings of the early times

We present excerpts from two texts of Chiara, from 1948 and 1950 respectively, both characterized by the wealth and ardent power of the charism in its early history. Chiara narrates how she and her companions came to understand chapter 17 of the Gospel of John. While different, these two accounts contain elements which remain constant. Firstly, Chiara expresses how deeply she understood and penetrated into John 17, which is evidenced by her use of the verbs understand, and comprehend, and the adjective luminous. Then we see the apostolic zeal that comes from this light and that bears abundant fruit, including that the world believes, as proof of Jesus' words "that the world may believe that you have sent me" (see Jn 17:21). These passages also reveal their goal of being one with Jesus as Jesus is one with the Father and, therefore, of being one among us, aware of the radical sacrifices that this choice involves.

"Those who love me will keep my word ... You shall love your neighbor as yourself." We looked at one another and decided without hesitation "to love one another in order to love Him."

The more we "live" the gospel, the more we understand it.

Before we had launched ourselves into living it, like children who throw themselves into playing, we realized that even though the Word of God was not totally obscure for us, neither was it alive in our intellect, nor sacred to our heart.

Every day was a new discovery of the gospel, which was our only book, the only light of our life.

We clearly understood that everything lies in love, that mutual love "had to" constitute Jesus' last appeal to those who had followed Him, that "consuming ourselves in one" would of necessity be Jesus' last prayer to the Father, supreme synthesis of the Good News.

Jesus knew that the Holy Trinity was eternal beatitude, and He, the Man-God who had come down to redeem humanity, wanted to bring all those He loved into the comm-Unity of the Three.

That was his homeland, that was the homeland of the brothers and sisters he had loved to the point of shedding his blood for them.

"To be consumed in one" was the program for our life in order to love Him. ...

The faith and love, that He lived in us, drew us close to all those He made us encounter every day, and this spontaneous love, freely given, attracted them to the same ideal.*

We never thought of "doing" apostolate. We didn't really like this word. Some people had abused it, tarnished it. We only wanted to love others, in order to love him.

And we soon realized that this was the real apostolate.

Seven, fifteen, one hundred, five hundred, one thousand, three thousand and more souls of every vocation, of every social condition. Every day the number grew of people attracted by Jesus among us.

Our humanity, put on the cross by the life of unity, attracted everyone to it.

Perfect unity was lived and is still living among those souls spread throughout the whole of Italy and beyond it.

---

* By Ideal, Chiara indicates the divine gift of light of the spirituality of unity as well as the acceptance of the new lifestyle that comes from it.

Not only spiritual unity in our passionate quest to be another Jesus, but also concrete unity.

Everything was put in common: objects, homes, assistance and money.

And there was peace, there was heaven on earth.

Life totally changed. ...

And all of this because the only beginning, the only middle, the only end was Jesus.

Jesus "in" us. Jesus "among" us.

Jesus, the purpose of time and of eternity.

Human minds grapple to find solutions to the dramatic events of our day. They will only find them in Jesus. Not only in Jesus who lives deep within each person, but in Jesus who reigns "among" souls.

They do not have time to discuss, because He very clearly shows to those who are united to others in his name, what "needs to be done" to give back real peace to the world.

There is a "porro unum necessarium" ("need of only one thing" [Lk 10:42]) for a soul to have in its relationship with God.

There is a "porro unum necessarium" for a soul to have a relationship with his or her neighbors, and this is to love them as oneself, to the point of becoming one here on earth, in anticipation of the perfect consummation of souls in *the* One, Jesus, in heaven.

This is the Christian community.

October, 1948[8]

21

The above (selections of the article in *Fides)* was the outcome of a meeting with Igino Giordani that we describe here. The honorable Igino Giordani* was impressed by the meeting he had with Chiara on September 17, 1948, in Montecitorio, site of the Italian Parliament. In order not to lose contact, he asked Chiara to write this piece for *Fides*, the monthly Vatican magazine that he directed. On that occasion, three religious of the Franciscan family had visited him together with Chiara. Giordani, whom Chiara later nicknamed "Foco," wrote that day in his diary "This morning at Montecitorio I was visited by angels: a Capuchin, a Friar Minor, a Conventual, and two Third Order members, one male, one female: Silvia Lubich, who is starting a community in Trent."[9]

---

* Igino Giordani (1894–1980), Servant of God, a member of the Italian Parliament and of the Constitutional Assembly, and a prominent civil and ecclesial personality, was also a writer and a journalist. He met Chiara Lubich (whose baptismal name was Silvia) in 1948. The Focolare Movement had already started, but because of his extraordinary work alongside Chiara over the years, she considered him one of the co-founders. His cause for canonization is currently being promoted.

Unity, *basis* of our every action

One day we understood how we must love one another: "Until we are consumed in one," as one of us said, until we fulfill, first among ourselves and then with those whom we loved, the Testament of Jesus, " ... that they may all be one."

We looked at the unity of the heavenly Father with the divine Son, and our "Idea" appeared to be so beautiful, that from that moment on, we called it "Unity." And "Movement of Unity" described how people of every type were directing their lives toward God in their practice of evangelical charity.

Unity was the basis of our every action (we sincerely loved one another before we acted in any way or for any reason.... The gospel asked us to be reconciled with our brothers and sisters before placing our gift on the altar!).

—It was the *means* to be able to love our neighbor (we made ourselves one with everyone. We cried with those who cried; we laughed with those who laughed, in order to love our neighbor as we loved ourselves; and the basis of everything was mutual and continuous charity, before any discussions, before our own interests, etc.).

—It was the *goal* because it had been the goal of Jesus' life, who died in order to bring mankind back to the one fold, of Jesus whom we all wanted to imitate whatever our vocation might be, because He is Light for everyone.

Trent, 1950

To Carry Out the Testament of Jesus

We all understood the need to bring this unity of spirits to our own surroundings and, as a result, the souls who belonged to the Community continued to grow in number: families were recomposed in peace; convents reclaimed their former fervor. ...

So from the fruits, the truth of the Words of Jesus was confirmed: "that they may all be one ... so that the world may believe that you have sent me" (Jn 17:21). ...

The gospel was fulfilled to the letter by God, the Father of everyone, as we tried, with the strength of unity, to resolve every issue in the light of the gospel taken literally.

And Providence was clearly manifested for all those who recognized in every situation the voice of God, the Father, who in his goodness makes everything work for their sanctity and for the fulfillment of His Kingdom. The atmosphere, which before had been cold, full of death and suffering, was now warm, for there was so much Light in everyone as a result of so much charity, and "there was not a needy person" among us. If one suffered, all suffered together. The unemployed found jobs, orphans had as many parents as fathers and mothers were present in the community, marriages were the bliss of paradise, because everyone participated in the joy of the others, thus multiplying it, while the numerous afflictions, shared by many, were almost wiped out. ...

It is therefore the realization of Jesus' Testament, in which all try to be one with Jesus as Jesus is one with the Father, and as a consequence, they are one among themselves. It is the gospel ideal taken into the midst of the world, as Jesus was in the midst of the world, and the Focolare Movement wishes to be an instrument in the hands of God for the purification of our surroundings by radiating charity.

God is Love and to radiate Love is to radiate God, and in order to radiate Him, we need to possess Him. God in us, therefore, God outside of us.

Thus we laid the foundation of the entire Movement, we remained faithful to the Ideal we chose at the beginning: God. God is Everything: he is the beginning and the end.

Trent, 1950

Jesus Crucified as the model

Unity costs sacrifice, the total death of our ego. That's why the souls who desire unity love Jesus Crucified as the model for their lives. To be crucified means to give up what we have, and who we are, in order to be like Him, since being another Him is the aspiration of all the people of the Focolare and the members of the community. There is no unity without him because love is sacrifice, is Jesus Crucified: "love one another as I have loved you."

Trent, 1950[10]

The root of the gift

From the outset, Chiara had the intuition that the source of the gift of unity was Jesus forsaken, who cries out "My God, my God, why have you forsaken me?" (Mk 15:34). She sees him as the one who assumed all separations, and took upon himself all the sufferings that we experience in our lives, in order to cancel them out and transform them into union with God. He is the principle and the foundation of unity. This certainty is repeatedly emphasized: Jesus endured the abandonment "to give us perfect unity." We offer these expressions taken from different letters of the early days.

Saint Clare! On this feast day of all the Franciscan saints, and our feast day too, may Saint Clare give you the fullness of her Seraphic Flame and her passionate love for Christ-Abandoned!

Keep Him ever before you as the example of utmost love.

He is Everything. He is the giver of *unity.*

November 29 (probably 1947)[11]

He [Jesus Forsaken] gave us Unity, the ideal which is God himself, the Holy Spirit, who joins the Father to the Son, and whose presence for a moment on the cross, Jesus Forsaken no longer felt, so that we would never feel abandoned by God! From that heart, spiritually torn apart and shattered by such great anguish that was infinitely greater than any physical wound, the Ideal burst forth.

March 13, 1948 [12]

We have chosen as the only purpose for our life, as our only goal, as our everything:

Jesus Crucified, who cries out: "My God, my God, why have you forsaken me?"

This is Jesus in his moment of maximum pain! Infinite disunity so that he can give perfect unity to

27

us, which we will reach only relatively here below and then completely in Paradise.

April 1, 1948[13]

2. A Lifetime Project

Reading Jesus' prayer in John 17, Chiara immediately understood that this is a lifetime project and a program to which she can dedicate her whole self. There is no doubt that when Chiara called this prayer the *Magna Carta*, or a lifetime program, she was drawing from the gift of unity to make the fundamental choice to live for unity. It was a radical decision that had to be kept always alive, and constantly in focus.

Charisms

[You have asked me a question:] How did this adventure of unity begin?

Dear friends, it began when not I, but Another wanted it.

You may know that from time to time certain gifts arrive on earth: they are called charisms.

They are bestowed by the One who governs history and guides it to a very precise objective: all good. And he channels towards this goal even whatever harm we, men and women, may cause in this world.

I am speaking of God, God who is Love, in whom many of us strongly believe.

One day, many years ago, one of these charisms came down here, too.

Because of this charism, young as we were at the time, we understood that a wonderful design had been bestowed on us, a task, almost a mission: to work, in the life which had been given to us, so that all may be one, setting in motion, in our hearts and in the hearts of others, love.

A dream? A utopia?

Certainly not, given that Jesus prayed to his Father in heaven with these precise words: "that they may all be one."

Could the Father (who is God), of a Son (who is God and with whom he is only one God), not hear his voice?

We set off then with confidence towards that goal, and now throughout the world there are millions and millions of us, including children, youth and adults, from almost every nation on earth. We can't count how many we are, it's an impossible task.

Rocca di Papa,
April 26, 1999*

---

* From a message to youth gathered in the little town of Loppiano (Florence).

Keep one idea fixed in your head: unity

Keep one idea fixed in your head.
It was always a single idea that made great saints.
And our idea is this:
Unity.
"Yes, Father!" We are Jesus! Likenesses of Jesus, responding in every present moment to *His will: Yes, Fath*er!

Yes, yes, yes, always and only yes.

This yes will make you share in our unity that exists only in God....

Unity: continual, direct communication with God through radical self-denial in the present moment, renouncing everything that is not God. I want only God. He alone is Everything!

Unity: among us, in this stupendous community of people scattered through the world, enclosed and sealed only by the love of God!

New Year's Eve, 1947*

What if unity were pronounced by the Almighty?

Unity: a divine word. If at any moment the Almighty were to pronounce this word, and people

* From a letter to the young women she followed.

everywhere were to apply it in the most varied ways, we would suddenly see the world stop in its tracks, and like a film running backwards, retake its course in the opposite direction. Countless people would reverse their tracks along the wide road to perdition and would convert to God, choosing the narrow road. ... Families separated by rifts, their hearts hardened by misunderstandings and hatred, and deadened by divorce, would be recomposed. Children would be born into an atmosphere of human and divine love, and new people would be shaped, giving promise to a more Christian future.

Factories, often a gathering of people who are "slaves" to their work in a bored, if not vulgar atmosphere, would become places of peace, where all do their share for the good of all. Schools would break through the limits of their short-lived knowledge, making every discipline a footstool for the contemplation of things eternal, learned in the classroom in a daily revelation of mysteries, intuited from basic formulas, simple laws, or even numbers. ...

And elected bodies would be transformed into meeting places for people who battle not so much for particular interests, but for the good of all, without deceiving other colleagues or countries.

We would see a world becoming kinder, as if, in a dream, heaven come down upon earth, and the harmonies of creation become the setting for the unity of hearts.

We would see. … But it is a dream! It seems like a dream!

Yet you asked for nothing less when you prayed: "Your will be done on earth as it is in heaven" (Mt 6:10).

1961[14]

Unity and nothing else

Whenever we are asked for a definition of our spirituality, or what difference there is between the gift of God to our Movement and the gifts with which he has decorated and enriched others in the Church today and throughout the centuries, we have no hesitation in replying: unity.

Unity is our specific vocation. Unity is what characterizes the Focolare. Unity and not other ideas or words that, in one way or another, can stand for splendid and divine ways of going to God, as, for instance, poverty for the Franciscan Movement, obedience perhaps for the Jesuits, the little way for followers of Thérèse of Lisieux, or prayer for the Carmelites of St. Teresa of Avila.

The word that epitomizes our spirituality is unity. For us, unity includes every other supernatural reality, every other practice or commandment, every other religious attitude.

October 5, 1981[15]

What characterizes us?

I feel the responsibility, for as long as I am alive, to point out clearly what is essential and what is secondary. ...

[All the] ideas, which are at the basis of our spirituality, are necessary if they are understood from our viewpoint, from what God has given to us.

So we, too, must choose God in the way He wants to be chosen. We must do the will of God, which for us is to have Jesus among us. We must love Jesus forsaken, who for us is the key to unity; and so on, all the points of our spirituality. This leads us to the conclusion that there is an idea which truly characterizes us, an idea which is really ours ... : this idea has a name — unity. This is really ours.

November 4, 1961[*]

Our only goal: to be consumed in one

Mutual love—we understood this one day as we were crossing a bridge (almost a symbol of a new way of going to God)—had to reach the point

[*] From a talk to young women who want to consecrate their lives to bring unity to the world.

of our being consumed in one, of making us experience unity.

Then there was the time in the cellar (that we all know about) when we read Jesus' testament, which appeared to us as the *Magna Carta* of what was coming to life.

And there was such a radical and total love for our neighbor that it made us lose sight of all other objectives (there was only that one!), even that of sanctity.... as it was understood at that time (an individual sanctity). If we, who were called to a new way, had followed the idea of sanctity as it was understood then, it would have been tarnished by self-love and egoism. For us, personal sanctity would result from our living unity.

Rocca di Papa,
October 1, 1994*

Our rock: Unity

With great joy and gratitude it seems that the Holy Spirit has suggested to us the way to ensure this [the growth of the Movement], both for now and in the future. It is a simple and convincing invention, with no price to pay.

---

* From a speech to directors of the Focolare Movement from around the world.

A statement made by Jesus offers us a full guarantee of this and gives us peace.

He states that a house built on the rock will not fall, unlike the one built on sand. Winds, storms and floods might come, but the house remains standing. The rock is the Word of God listened to and put into practice.

The Work of Mary,* too, can be compared to a house which is being built up in the world.

For this house, too, there will be salvation, safety, stability and progress if it is based on the Word of God, if those who build it want nothing other than to live the Word.

But what is the word that the Spirit imprinted like a seal on this house, on our Movement, when heaven conceived the idea and began to bring it about here on earth?

We know it. The word is "Unity." Unity is the word that summarizes our entire spirituality: unity with God, unity with our neighbors. Or better, unity with our neighbors in order to attain union with God. ...

Our statutes put unity at the basis of everything, as the norm of all norms, the rule to be observed before any other rule. It is *the* word for us; it is the rock.

We have no meaning in life if not in this word, where everything makes sense—our every action, every prayer, every breath. And if we concentrate on

---

* The Focolare Movement is also called "Work of Mary."

this word, if we live it as well as we can, everything will be safeguarded for us: both we ourselves and that part of the Movement entrusted to us.

Perhaps in the future the Work of Mary as a whole or in its various zones [around the world] will go through moments quite different from the one we are experiencing now, which is marked by many consolations, fruits, light and fire. There may come moments of darkness, of anguish, there might arise persecutions, temptations. The devil, through a thousand different means, could try to destroy everything; there might be misfortunes or catastrophes ... but if we stand firm on the rock of unity nothing will be able to touch us; everything will go ahead just as before.

Rocca di Papa,
November 9, 1989[*16]

---

*   This collection includes a few texts of Chiara's comments during telephone conference calls. The idea began in August 1980 to gather periodically the members of the Focolare Movement around the world for a moment of planetary communion. Chiara would communicate, from the place where she was that day, a spiritual thought, based on experience. An update of the main events of the Movement in that period would follow. This planetary meeting still exists today.

What does God want from us?

I'd like to tell you something that is really in my heart.

During these days we've all been living for ... Mother Teresa.* Mother Teresa was a great friend of mine ... We had a very close and profound friendship. It was twenty years ago when she asked to meet me. She came to the Mariapolis Center, I welcomed her and she said to me: "Tell me about your Ideal." ...

I admired her for many things, especially for her holiness, her heroism, but in a very special way, I admired her determination. This is what I feel I have to learn from Mother Teresa, taking her as my model in this: her determination. She had an ideal and she never diverted from it. Her ideal was the poorest of the poor and she never diverted (from this). ...

We must learn to have this determination, this absolute resolve, this integrity; we must have it too. What does God want from us? From us God wants *ut omnes unum sint*, ["that they may all be one"] which we will achieve through the four dialogues: through an ever deeper communion at the heart of

---

* Mother Teresa of Calcutta, who died on September 5th of that year. Founder of the Missionaries of Charity, she was a figure universally recognized for her charitable works. She was beatified by Pope John Paul II on October 19, 1993.

the Catholic Church among all the faithful, among the parishes, the dioceses, always more communion, increasing the feeling that we are all brothers and sisters, working all together for what is the good, esteeming everyone, helping everyone, etc.

And then we must work for the new reality that we bring, which you already know about, I think, which is the ecumenism of the people. We spoke about it in Graz[*7] and those who were present there felt that they were only one people, even though they belonged to different Churches. It is the second dialogue that we carry forward in the field of ecumenism.

And then love for other religions, that is, for the faithful of other religions, so as to arrive at universal brotherhood with them, too.

And finally, also dialogue with people who do not have any particular religious belief, but are persons of great culture with wonderful values.

September 23, 1997[†]

---

[*] On June 28, 1997, Chiara spoke to the Second European Ecumenical Assembly in Graz, Austria before an audience of 3,000 people. She challenged each one to be a "leader of love." A bishop defined that moment like this: "A new phase for ecumenism, an action plan for all the people of God."

[†] From a dialogue with a large group of people from different social, cultural and ecclesial backgrounds who were committed to living out and spreading the spirituality of unity, Rimini.

Chapter 2

Unity is Unity with God and the Design of God on History

The texts presented in this chapter examine in depth unity in its truest meaning. For Chiara, unity is, first of all, an encounter with Jesus and the experience that we can make of his Person. Other texts illustrate how unity is unity with God, unity in God; indeed it is no less than the design of God on history.

1. Unity in One Word: It's a Person

Ineffable, indescribable, intangible, untouchable, omnipotent, all Spirit: this is what unity is for Chiara. Unity is an experience— even amid serious trials—and Chiara cannot give it any other definition: it is Jesus.

Oh! Unity, Unity! What divine beauty! We have no human words to say what it is!

It is Jesus!

August 6, 1947[17]

Unity! Who would dare speak of it?

It is as ineffable as God.

You feel it, see it, rejoice over it ... but it is ineffable!

All enjoy its presence, all suffer its absence.

It is peace, joy, love, ardor, and the spirit of heroism, of boundless generosity.

It is Jesus among us!

April 29, 1948[18]

Unity: wonder and gift

At the beginning of June 1948, the Archbishop of Trent, Most Reverend Carlo De Ferrari, received a series of formal charges against the nascent Movement and as a result he opened an investigation. The blow could be fatal, so Chiara speaks in this letter of unity that is given or is taken away. In spite of the possibility of destruction "after six years of building," this trial is already a victory because it brings her closer to the heart of unity that is Jesus.

The investigation concluded favorably for the Movement on July 14th of that year and the Archbishop said a few days later: "All the works of God are strongly challenged but they end up being fortified after the struggle. This has happened to you, too. Yours is a work of God."

In these days of acute suffering and incredible joy, I've seen, felt, and experienced with my soul that Unity is not the Focolares, the Crusade,* the distance, approvals or disapprovals. Unity is Something beyond all these things. It's Heavenly Peace—it's complete Joy—it's perfect Light that illuminates the thickest darkness—it's pure and ardent Love ... it's Jesus.

And He is enough for us.

We see now, and we'll see in the future perhaps, everything falling apart. This would be the logical consequence of what has occurred in these days. "Logical" according to the finite vision of men, but not according to God who can—with an amazing miracle—salvage everything and make all things new.

And amid all this destruction—after six years of building—nothing will have been taken away from us. Love is at the center of our heart, intact, stronger, more beautiful and true, more our one and only, love is in the center of our Kingdom of souls!

Those who felt fearful before now draw near to us because they feel *safe*. The timid ones are

---

* At the end of January 1947, having come across some unsigned brochures entitled, *Unity: ut unum sint,* Chiara met Fr. Leone Veuthey, O.F.M. Conv., who was distributing them. Father Veuthey had begun a "charity crusade" in which for three years Chiara and those who followed her willingly participated. He would later refer to them as the apostles from Trent where "300 persons were prepared to take up the crusade."

now waiting to see the results in order to then say that they were on the side of those who won! How many—especially those in the focolares— feel stronger now, attached to the Rock which is *Jesus*—ready even to die for Him. And *Unity*, this impalpable, untouchable, invisible Something *rises up and dominates*! All spiritual—all Spirit! And yet *Real, Concrete, satisfying the soul and making it sing.*

Oh, Father! What a Way the Lord has given us! How wondrous! What a gift!

If you only knew what is happening among us and within us.

Satan's repeated attempts to make everything fall apart are proof of how much this Work matters to God.

But Satan can't get away with it.

God is invincible!

They give us Unity, we have God!

They take away Unity, we have Christ on a cross who cries: "My God, my God, why have you abandoned me?"

Trent, June 15, 1948[19]

Above all, be one

Be attentive to Satan's attacks on Unity. I speak from experience: he'll try everything to destroy Unity. He knows Unity is omnipotent and that the souls consumed in One are absolutely lost to him.

And so, "above all" (even if this "all" includes the most beautiful things, the most sacred things, like praying, celebrating the Holy Mass, etc, etc.) be one! Then it will no longer be you who acts, prays, or celebrates ... but always Jesus in you!

Unity is the training ground for sanctity. It's the triumph of charity. It's already Paradise experienced, even though we are still on this earth, and therefore, always "on the battlefield" to maintain our unity, to be *one* and to consume other souls in *one*! ...

Have everything in common: give all that you have to each other with generosity! Then, one by one, Jesus will consume the brothers who live with you, and will prepare those who are far away for Unity.

Trent, December 27, 1948[20]

Unity shows the Risen Lord to the world

Q:—Can you tell us what unity means for you now, thirty-eight years after God bestowed on you this charism?

I noticed, after thirty-eight years, that unity is something really important. ...

What is unity for me?

Jesus, who rose from the dead, said: "I am with you always, to the end of the age." Therefore, Jesus is right here, where there is unity, the Risen Lord is right here, among us. Yes, He is here. And we ought to love one another so much that we show Him to the world, draw Him forth, display Him, express Him: we must be like the monstrance of the risen Jesus. Do you understand? This is our task.

So, to sum up: for me unity is Jesus risen in the world today. This is the task of our Movement. It's a huge thing! To show Him, to make Him visible, as the Virgin Mary showed baby Jesus.

Seoul, January 2, 1982[*]

---

[*] From a dialogue with a large group of people from Korea, of different social and cultural backgrounds and ecclesial commitments, who are active in living out and spreading the spirituality of unity.

Unity, Jesus among us, is the fullness of joy

I would like us to take a deeper look at this grace [of unity], to analyze it more closely.

What is it, who is it?

We know the answer. It's certainly not a simple point of our spirituality. Unity brings into our midst a person, a person who is God Himself. Unity is Jesus among us.

A Father of the Church says that unity is that "accord" between several people in thought and in sentiment, so as to arrive at that concord which "unites and contains the Son of God." [21]

And His presence — we can bear witness to this — is the source of profound happiness: Jesus among us is the fullness of joy; He makes our lives and the lives of all those who live unity an unceasing celebration.

Rocca di Papa,
October 24, 1996 [22]

2. Unity is First of All, Unity with God

In the thought of Chiara, unity is first of all unity with God, so as to become "another Jesus." To reach this goal, she presents many pathways: to do the will of God as He did, to pray, to deny ourselves in order to love the others, etc. In order to reach union with God, Chiara gives a privileged place to the

Eucharist, the bond of unity. We explain these pathways only briefly because the same topic is already presented in other books of this series.

Jesus: our model

The soul must aim at being, as soon as possible, another Jesus.

Just as in Jesus, human and divine nature were only one thing, in the same way the soul must aim at fusing into one the human and divine aspects contained within it.

Act "as Jesus" did here on earth. Imitate him as a mirror reflects features and gestures.

Be "the mirror" of Jesus.

Put our human nature at God's disposal so that he can use it to make his beloved Son live again in us.

To achieve this, do only the Will of the Father, as Jesus did.

To be able to have always on our lips the words that Jesus said about himself.

Before all else, the soul must always fix its gaze on the *one* Father of many children.

Then it must see all as children of the same Father. . . .

Jesus, our model, taught us two things alone, which are *one*: to be children of only one Father and to be brothers and sisters to each other.

When all these children will carry out the will of the one Father — as Jesus did — then they will be only one thing.

And the Will of the Father is contained in the Gospel, and it is: to be one with God the Father through Jesus and following his example; and to be one with all our brothers and sisters. That they may all be one.

When a soul re-lives Christ in its decisive and total obedience to the Father, then in that soul there will be unity.

December 2, 1946[23]

To be, and then to speak and act

Our new evangelization — which, in practice, corresponds to a more decisive spreading of the Ideal — consists first in *living*, in *giving witness* with our life to what we will then proclaim; in other words, in *being* before speaking.

But being what?

Being, each of us, one with God, through union with Him which is expressed in making the whole day a prayer, as we have often explained, and in the prayers indicated in our Statutes.

Being one with God by doing His will, and one with our brothers and sisters in whom He is present, especially the "least."

And being *one with one another*, which is in itself a way of speaking, of crying out, of proclaiming to the world: "that they may all be one ... so that the world may believe" (Jn. 17:21).

In short, to be in action the Testament of Jesus which sums up the entire Gospel.

To be!

Switzerland,
August 29, 1991[24]

Only two* Saints can Form a Perfect Unity

I write to this *unity* of two souls already fused together in one single and burning desire.

What joy! In his immense goodness, Jesus grants that I find not only one heart, but two, for He knows that a *perfect Unity of two hearts cannot but be formed by Saints and that only two Saints can form a perfect Unity.*

Here is my advice:

---

* Chiara responds to a letter she probably received from two religious sisters and vigorously corrects them with love.

1. To boldly reach your goal, you must aim at only one thing (which has a second part to it that comes as a consequence): *uniting yourselves to Jesus.*

2. Unite your hearts to each other with such supernatural love that it will overcome every divergence, every difficulty, every obstacle that could arise between you. And extend this love to all your sisters.

October 3, (1946?)[25]

Unity among us is achieved if each one is well united to God, in accordance with our charism. It is written in fact, "As you, Father, are in me and I am in you, may they also be in us" (see Jn 17:21). Unity, therefore, is first of all personal union with God, but in accordance with our way of thinking. This unity with God means everything: it means to be holy, to be perfect, to reach the highest stage of prayer. Jesus said, "If any want to become my followers, [that is, to be another him and reach union with the Father], let them deny themselves and take up their cross and follow me." Through our charism we attain self-denial by going out of ourselves and loving others.

Castel Gandolfo,
January, 30 1990[26]

Only God with God can achieve unity

Our solitude with God and our life of unity with our brothers and sisters are both essential, precisely to be sure of a true solitude with God and a true life of unity with our brothers and sisters.

Solitude, which is closing in on ourselves, even with the most holy of intentions, is not solitude with God. God is Father and loves you as he loves all the others and wants to see his family always united.

Solitude with God means letting God live in you so that, even when you are alone with him, all the others are present in the love that you carry in your heart.

On the other hand, the life of unity among Christians is not true if it is not made of "many" Jesuses, many people who no longer live but Christ lives in them, God in them.

Unity does not exist in other ways. Only God with God can achieve unity.

June 1975[27]

Unity and the Eucharist

Ours is the Ideal of unity. Now, is it not significant that Jesus, in his famous prayer to the Father, should ask for unity among his disciples and among those to come, right after having instituted the Eucharist which made that unity possible?

This is how Jesus prayed while walking towards the Garden of Olives: "Holy Father, protect them in your name that you have given me, so that they may be one, as we are one ... I ask not only on behalf of these but also on behalf of those who will believe in me through their word, that they may all be one. As you, Father, are in me and I in you, may they also be in us, so that the world may believe that you sent me. The glory that you have given me I have given them, so that they may be one, as we are one, I in them and you in me, that they may become completely one ..." (Jn 17:20–23).

If we love our ideal, our vocation to unity, we will passionately love the Eucharist.

Rocca di Papa,
October 8, 1976[28]

3. Unity is Unity in God Trinity

The Unity which is not founded on Jesus is a utopia

Q:—We notice often that the youth who leave Loppiano* are deeply convinced that a united world is possible because they experienced it. In your recent message to young people, you emphasized the idea that the Word must be the foundation of every activity. How can we convey the Word adequately?

By telling these young people that an ideal of unity which is not based on Jesus is a utopia.

I remember what a journalist told me with great sincerity in Tokyo: "You speak of unity. This can't only mean unity with God, but also unity among people. But how can we think of unity among different races, nationalities, religions and cultures? It sounds impossible." And he was totally right.

So I had to say that Jesus has the patent for this because he's the Son of God and he brought

---

*   This refers to young people who may attend one of several schools in Loppiano. There are schools for focolarine and focolarini (members who are consecrated in the Focolare in order to spread the spirit of unity) lasting 2 years with a third year held in a similar international center in Montet Switzerland; and "pre-schools" for vocational discernment and study of the Italian language; and schools for the Gen, young people involved with Focolare, lasting from 6 months to a year.

on earth something that didn't exist before; and that he alone could think of it because he brought charity, love. Therefore, he can achieve unity.

So, we can't mislead the youth by speaking of a romantic or platonic unity. We need to speak of the true unity and say that the ideal of unity is a utopia, a real utopia, and that it is only possible because Jesus spoke about it, he took it as his own because he is the Son of God. And only by being in him, like him, can we speak of unity. That's why we say: to be like him, to be in him, we must "eat" his words, because one of the effects of (living) his words is that we become another him. So, if we become another Jesus, we reason like him and say: unity is possible.

When we look at reality in a supernatural way, when we look at things with the eyes of Jesus, then all the marches for peace (or for other reasons) that we organize, or collecting signatures for peace, or raising money and funds, all of these activities have value because they rest on Jesus, they are done by Jesus, by "other" Jesuses. If they were accomplished by men and women, they would be out of proportion with the goal. The goal is too big.

Once someone asked me: "This *ut omnes unum sint*, Chiara, what is it, how can we bring it to fulfillment? It's impossible." And I had to tell him: "No, we are not the ones to accomplish it, but if we are Jesus we can contribute to its fulfillment. It won't be today, it won't be tomorrow, but it will be fulfilled."

February 19, 1986*

The Word of God lived out causes unity

The Word *makes us one*: it causes unity. Just as in grafting plants the two living parts of branches that are stripped of their bark come into contact and become one; likewise, when two souls, "stripped" of all that is merely human by living the Word of Life, come into contact, they too are better consumed into one.

Those who don't live the Word of God bring wherever they go a human atmosphere, an earthly one; not only do they not leaven the mass, but sometimes they depress it to the point of becoming a source of disagreement or division. It's what Cyprian feared, in his treatise *De unitate*, in which, while addressing especially the unity of the Church, he makes constant appeals to living the gospel, given that precisely because it was not being lived, there were schisms in the Church.

Morges, Switzerland, October 29, 2002†

---

* From a dialogue with the residents of the little town of Loppiano (near Florence, Italy). Founded in 1964, Loppiano is home to around 850 inhabitants from around 65 nations, welcoming thousands of visitors each year.
† From a speech to a congress of bishops of various Church-

Doing the will of God brings about unity

Look at the sun and its rays.

The sun is a symbol of the will of God, which is God himself. The rays are the will of God for each individual.

Walk towards the sun in the light of your ray, different and distinct from every other ray, and fulfill the particular, wonderful plan God wants from you.

There is an infinite number of rays, all coming from the same sun: a single will, particular for each person.

The closer the rays come to the sun, the closer they come to one another.

We too, the closer we come to God, by doing the will of God more and more perfectly, the closer we come to one another.

Until we are all one!

October 26 or 27, 1947[29]

es eager to examine in depth the life and doctrine of the spirituality of unity.

4. Unity is a Grace That Comes from Above

Only Jesus among us can fulfill his Testament

We always knew it was impossible for Jesus to bestow such a great ideal, to speak of such a great ideal, to poor human beings as we are. He spoke of unity among humankind as it is in the Holy Trinity, on the model of the Holy Trinity, and so to be more certain, he prayed to His Father, but this is also a guarantee that this prayer has already been answered.

Today I think I can say, after this Mariapolis, that if it is true that Jesus could not address this prayer to any human being, it is also true that no person can implement his Testament in this world, no disciple or saint will ever be capable of it, only he, he among us, will be the one who fulfills his testament, who will make of many, one.

Grottaferrata,
July 25, 1960[*]

---

[*] From a speech to a congress for people who wished to examine the spirituality of unity in depth. This meeting was entitled "Mariapolis School."

A grace that comes from above

Q:—On several occasions you have spoken to us, Chiara, of a mysticism and asceticism from the perspective of the spirituality of communion, which are necessary for experiencing unity. Can you tell us something more about these two aspects?

In order to achieve unity we must love one another, making every effort to be ready to die for one another. But while Jesus did not command anyone to unity, he prayed to his Father for unity because he knew that to reach full unity, our asceticism — loving one another — would not be enough. A grace from above is necessary and the grace comes to us through the Eucharist. The Eucharist is the bond of unity because it does everything. ... So, therefore, our effort is always necessary, hoping and waiting with confidence that then Jesus will do the rest through the Eucharist.

Madrid, December 8, 2002*

---

* From a dialogue with a large group of people from Spain, of different social and cultural backgrounds and ecclesial commitments who are active in living out and spreading the spirituality of unity.

5. Unity is God's Design on History

The prayer of Jesus for unity is universal

We think, sometimes, that when he said "that they may all be one," Jesus intended the unity of the world. It is not so. It could not be so because, while a certain number of people are consumed in one, even if there are many, some people die and others are born. Jesus' *"ut omnes"* refers to those who are his own. He wants, he asks that all those who are his be one. However, the universal element is implicit in this prayer because it exists in Jesus' mind. In fact, he said: "Go into all the world and proclaim the good news to the whole creation." Hence, he wants all peoples to become his and therefore wants the unity of all peoples.

Rocca di Papa, May 23, 1984,
Delivered in Istanbul on June 15, 1984[*]

---

[*] From a set of prepared answers to questions by people from Turkey who were familiar in various ways with the experience and the spirituality of unity.

Unity is the summary of Revelation

From that moment on [after reading the prayer for unity], through this new charism which was later defined as "the charism of unity," we understood the gospel, all the gospel, from one very precise angle, from unity. In fact, the prayer of unity is a summary of Christ's divine desires and for this reason it can be defined as the "summary of the gospel." We saw the gospel and the New Testament, in general, completely in function of unity: Jesus had lived and spoken, He had died and risen so that all Christians would be one in Him and through Him in the Father, and one with one another.

Zurich, September 10, 1994[*]

Unity is God's design for humanity

Q:—Chiara, what does it mean to you to write the themes on unity?

Beginning to go more deeply into this subject … I realized that the charism God has given to the Movement is rather special. I really feel that I must sincerely say this.

---

[*] From a speech to an ecumenical conference entitled "Living the Gospel Together."

Unity is not a virtue as poverty can be ... as obedience can be ... as chastity can be, humility, and so on. Unity is the very design that God has for humanity from when humanity began until the end, when Jesus will return. It is God's plan for humanity.

Therefore, it is all God's will ... and all God's will is concentrated there, in unity.

Loppiano, June 22, 1981*

---

* From a dialogue with young people who want to consecrate their lives to bring unity to the world. Chiara had prepared a few talks on the subject of unity to be delivered during the month of October of that year.

Chapter 3

Unity in Paradise '49, a prophetic and founding experience

During the summer of 1949, while spending a period of rest with some of her companions in the Dolomite Mountains, Chiara received such illuminations and revelations that, as she would recall later, religion appeared new to her: "We understood better many truths of the faith."[30]

Love for Jesus crucified and forsaken was the background of that period. In fact, the preceding months had been pervaded by His mystery. Chiara lived it intensely in communion with others and understood it always more deeply. Jesus sums up the whole of the gospel; He is the "summary" of all sufferings, all loves, all virtues.[31] Their vacation in the mountains ends with a passage dated September 20, 1949, with a significant title: "I have only one spouse on earth, Jesus Forsaken,"[32] which marks a decisive step forward in making a more conscious choice to follow Him.

It is unity, however, inseparable from the reality of Jesus forsaken, which marks the beginning of that period called "Paradise '49." On July 16th of that year, a new fact took place which proved to be filled with consequences for a collective mystical experience: a "Pact of Unity" between Chiara and Igino Giordani (Foco),[*] which was soon broadened to include the other companions, and whose detailed account is presented in the first text of this chapter. It was a period in which unity is lived in a dimension that anticipates what it will be at the end of times: "We were fused—into one soul—by the love of God."[33] "In the fire of the Trinity, we had been so fused into one that I called our company 'Soul.' We were the Soul." [34]

We will offer a sampling now of some passages of a mystical nature, from that period, or related to that time, on the subject of unity.

The pact with Igino Giordani

Igino Giordani (Foco), driven by a strong spiritual need of union with God, asks Chiara to make a vow of obedience to her. She doesn't think such a vow was in harmony with her spirituality but, attentive not to squander what could have been an inspiration, she proposes to Foco to allow Jesus be the one to build the bond that He wants between them, along these terms: "You know my life.

---

[*]   "Foco," meaning "fire," was a nickname given to Giordani by Chiara.

I am nothing. I want to live, in fact, as Jesus Forsaken who made himself completely nothing. You too are nothing because you live in the same manner. So then, tomorrow we will go to church and to Jesus-Eucharist who will come into my heart, as in an empty chalice, I will say: 'On the nothingness of me, please make a pact of unity with Jesus Eucharist in the heart of Foco. And do it, Jesus, in such a way that what comes out is the kind of bond between us that you have in mind.'" Then I added: "And you Foco, do the same."[35] The chronicle of the pact that we present now dates from twelve years after the facts, when Chiara believed that the writings of that period had been destroyed.

Foco, taken by the desire to serve God, proposed making a vow of obedience to me.

I did not see any need for this, nor was this desire in harmony with my Ideal that was "to live according to the Mystical Body" (for me the greatest expression of Christian life). But so as not to waste this act of love of his that he wanted to make for the Lord, I proposed to change it.

The following morning, during Holy Communion, both of us would pray to Jesus-Eucharist that, on *our nothingness*, He should make a pact of unity.

We did this with full faith and with love.

While Foco then went to visit the fathers of the monastery next to the church, I went before the Blessed Sacrament to pray to Jesus. But I found it impossible. I could not utter the word *Jesus*, because it would have been calling upon Someone I realized had become identified with me, One who in that moment I was.

I had the impression of finding myself on the peak of a very high mountain, seemingly the highest one possible, that came to a point, the point of a pin: *one* therefore, and high, but *not love* (and from this came my instantaneous torment), so much that it seemed to me that even *being God, but not triune*, would have been hell.

And in that instant, on my lips blossomed the word "Father" and I found communion again in the midst of amazement and joy.

I told Foco about this and, I do not know in which moment of that day, I found myself again, as in a vision seen with the eyes of the soul, having come into the Bosom of the Father, who showed me, as it were, the inside of a sun that was all gold or flames of gold, infinite, but not frightening.

I remember well that this vision — let's call it — only became clear to me when I asked the *pope** on the nothingness of themselves, to make

---

*   This is a word in the dialect from the region of Trent, here in its feminine form, meaning "children." Chiara uses it to refer to the women who lived with her in the focolare house. The term recalls the "little ones," the "children" of the gospel.

the same pact with Jesus-Eucharist, so as to be united with us.

And I saw this little company of persons in the sun.

From that moment, I called "Soul" that One which united all of us. And for two months, while there was a succession of intellectual and imaginary visions (as it seems to me they were, though I could be grossly mistaken),* we always spoke of the Soul.

Within it we had the impression of finding ourselves in Heaven. Above all there was space to breathe that was infinite, ample, utterly new, and our souls found themselves at ease.

In the Communions we received on the following days, the "Soul" was aware of being in communion with God and, therefore, of taking steps forward in the divine. And during the day these "Realities," as we called them and felt them to be, were lived by all of us united in a rather unique way, perhaps as a result of these special graces.

In the evening, at our meditation that lasted about half an hour, we were careful to place the whole of our souls in the most absolute passivity, so that the Lord, if he wished, could communicate Himself. And my companions silenced everything in them, even what could have been inspirations, so that unity with me would be perfect.

---

* Using the theological language of the time, Chiara indicates the ways in which God discloses himself in mystical experience, either by "visions" created by God in the imagination or by "communications" in the intellect.

And during the meditation new manifestations followed one after another. I was always intent upon communicating them at once to the other *pope*, because I felt them to be our common heritage and because we could then all place ourselves in those Realities.

Oberiberg, June 30, 1961[36]

We will only be Word of God

In Heaven we will be solely Word of God and in the unity of our souls there will be the harmony of the new song which is the Gospel formed by the Mystical Body of Christ. Each one of us will be a Word, but, since each Word is the whole Word, each one of us will be the Word, will be a harmony = a unity. The new song is the harmony of harmonies! The song of the Trinity.

From a written passage, July 20, 1949

Those who live unity see the gospel with the eye of God and penetrate there in depth, more or less, in proportion to their experience, that is, to the holiness gathered in their life of unity, and the intensity with which they live the present moment.

From a written passage, May 16, 1950

Unity and disunity in the afterlife

Here below [on earth] people were attached to that which passes.... There below [in the afterlife] they find again that which is empty and vain and dead and pain and cold and fire, everything that can hurt by burning and freezing, because it will be a cold (gnashing of teeth) that never makes unity with fire (eternal fire) and therefore never lukewarm, since in hell two things can never love one another. There will be all things, but still, immobile. There will also be the one who runs, but never stopping. Either motion alone or quietude alone. Never the unity of opposites, because unity would be life.

From a written passage, July 24, 1949

Love, unity and Trinity

To be incorporated in Christ does not mean only that we be a member and He the head, but also to be all one with Him, a perfect unity between head and member: a single Flesh, a single Blood, a single Soul and Divinity. The principle of Life remains always in Him, but we are all one with Him: as in the Trinity.

From a written passage, December 17, 1949

Love cannot be expressed because it is *Unity*.

To unfold a paper fan means to open it, to take away the creases. Love cannot be unfolded because it is Unity.

The Trinity is God "unfolded" in Three. But each is Trinity: all God.

Jesus alone could "unfold" Love because in each Word of his was Unity. Each one is all God: Love and Truth. Each Word of life is Jesus.

From a written passage, September 22, 1951

In that empty soul [of Jesus forsaken], the Light of God was unfolded like a fan and penetrated into each soul—if it was open—in ways that are various yet one, as colors are various yet of the same luminous substance. It didn't illuminate two souls equally — as the Three in the Trinity are not equal but distinct Persons — and to each bestowed its beauty so that they be desirable and lovable by the others, and in love (which was the common substance in which they recognized themselves as one and each one in the other) be recomposed in the One who had re-created them with his Light, which is He himself.

And that Light which touched each one made human nature divine, made nature supernatural, and, through human beings, all that is created.

Thus everything is advancing towards God and nothing will be lost.

From a written passage,
Fregene, October 15, 1949

Ascetics and mystics

The following text (written sometime between 1949 and 1951) focuses on the presence of Jesus in the midst of his people. Chiara inserted it in a talk she gave in the year 2000 to various groups of persons consecrated in the Focolare, because, she said, it illustrates the asceticism and the mysticism of the life in unity. The passage is addressed to an unknown person.

Being united in the name of Jesus means both being united for Him, that is, to carry out his command (his will), and being united as He wants.

Therefore, when we come together even for reasons that are beautiful, even spiritual, but which are not in his name, He is not among us. For example, if I meet with a friend in the name of friendship or in order to do some kind of work together or for entertainment, Jesus is not among us. If I were a consecrated religious leaving with another brother for a mission, Jesus would not yet be among us.

Jesus is among us when we are united in him, in his will, which is in He himself, and his will is to love one another as he loved us.

The words of Jesus: "For where two or three are gathered in my name, I am there among them," must be considered together with "Love one another as I have loved you." ...

Therefore, the two of us, for example, are united in the name of Jesus if we love one another as he loved us.

Now, from this you will understand how even we who live in the focolare do not always have Jesus in our midst. To have him among us, in every moment I would have to love you (presuming that it is just the two of us who live in a particular focolare) as he loved us, and be loved in return by you *in the same way.*

He loved us to the point of dying for us, and to the point of suffering even the abandonment.

Not always, or rarely, does love for our neighbor require such sacrifice. However, if the love that I must have for you (that action which is an expression of love) does not contain *intentionally* the way of loving with which He loved us, I do not love as He loves. Similarly, if you do not love to this extent, then you are not loving in this way either, and so we are *not* united in his name and Jesus is *not* among us.

You see, for him to be present, this is how we must love one another. But you know that loving in this way means being "another Jesus." Now, for him to be present among us, it is necessary that we already "be" Him beforehand.

But it is a "before" that is also an "after."

In fact, we are not perfectly him until he is in our midst.

When he is among us we are ONE and we are THREE, each equal to the one.

In essence, we can sense when he is present among us: when we feel that we are free, one, full of light and joy. When torrents of living water flow from within us.

This happens when two are united in the name of Jesus. They must first be Jesus in order to have Him among them, but they are fully Jesus when they have Him among them.

When we are united and He is present, we are no longer two, but *one*. In fact, what I say in that moment, it is not I who say it, but I, Jesus, and you in me. And when you speak, it is not you, but you, Jesus, and I in you. We are a single Jesus and we are also distinct: I (with you in me and Jesus), you (with me in you and Jesus), and Jesus among us in whom there are you and I.

And His presence in our midst is a mystical presence among us.

And He is in the Father; therefore, in Him, the two of us are in the Father and we participate in the life of the Trinity.

And the Trinitarian Life flows freely in us, and as we love the others as He has loved us, we bring them to participate in this treasure of divine Life.

Or rather, they experience within themselves the treasure which they already had in God through Jesus because of Baptism and the other sacraments.

The novelty of this Light (a practical novelty) is that not only must we not be parasites of Jesus among us, but it is not even possible to do so, meaning to live comfortably off him passively awaiting his Light. In fact, He is not among us when we are not Him. It is necessary, therefore, that we direct all our efforts toward being like Him, while still awaiting passively that He might come among us so that we can be Him fully.

Here lies the splendid simplicity of our Ideal which is also divine and mysterious.

Living Christianity means being completely active and completely passive: the unity of opposites: *God*.

From a written passage, undated

The way of Unity

Those who enter the way of unity, enter into Jesus. They put themselves aside in order to live Jesus. Actually, because they can only do one thing, they do not even put themselves aside; they go straight to living Jesus.

And those who live Jesus do not find themselves on a way, but on *the* Way. It is the Way in which the other ways (purgative, illuminative and unitive), working Trinitarianly, are united to one another; they join into one. Those who live Jesus are purified by this very fact, and are so enlightened so as to be his very same Light.

Those who enter the way of unity do not climb a mountain with exhausting effort, but through an initial and total commitment, made out of a love that brings about a death to their own selves, a total emptying of themselves, of their entire humanity into God (and only total emptying is love), come to find themselves instead already at the top of the mountain. It is impossible to go any higher and it is rest ("Come to me ... and I will give you rest" [Mt 11:28]). Their journey begins on the mountain crest going all the way to God, always starting again, in the same way as before, if they should stop.

Those who enter the way of unity live as children of God right from the very start. They are perfect as the Father right from the start, as the Child Jesus was perfect while he was still a child. Their growth is more like a manifestation that could be compared to that of a tree. While the tree is no more perfect than the seed that contained it, it is the manifestation of what the seed contained.

The gospel does not really speak about climbing. It says instead: "No one who puts a hand to the plow and looks back ..." [see Lk 9:62]. It speaks more about "entering," which presupposes a road, but on that road carrying a yoke that is easy and light.

It would be like traveling on a ray of the sun. Each one of the sun's rays is still the sun itself, but its light grows in intensity the closer it gets to the sun. It is similar for those who live unity. They live by allowing themselves to penetrate always more into God. They grow always closer to God, who lives in their hearts, and the closer they get to him, the closer they get to the hearts of their brothers and sisters. Those who live unity are already purified and enlightened. They are an expression of living purity, in the widest sense of the word, and of living light. Those who live unity are living gospels, and by living Jesus they live these three words of his:

– Those who live the word are already purified (see Jn 15:3);

– I will manifest myself to the one who loves me (see Jn 14:21);

– Those who remain united to me bear much fruit (see Jn 15:5).

They are three different ways, but lost in one, each way having the same value as the other. They are three, but one. And yet they are not just three, because they also contain all the other words of Jesus, and therefore, all the effects of the gospel.

From a written passage,
Rome, May 16, 1950[37]

Prayer in community

And, if the Heavens of the souls meet and *unite* in true unity, God is there. Otherwise, He is not. It's useless to call Him or hope for Him.

Thus I see clearly how there must be prayer in community (for example, when two people pray the rosary).

One soul prays to God in the other and the other in the first, since the two are a single soul, and the Trinity remains in it, being differentiated into Father and Son.

Thus the recollection is perfect and prayer a total embrace of Heaven and earth, because in that brother or sister I love the Brother, and therefore all the brothers and sisters and in them, as we have seen, all creation.

From a written passage, September 22, 1951

In the way of unity "you feel," in the sense that you notice whether there is unity or not. In fact, the way of unity is also mystical.

And in the same way you feel (as if the soul had the senses) if there is unity between your own soul and another, so in prayer we feel if our soul is intimate with God.

From a written passage, November 9, 1949

The mystical rose

We present this text in which Chiara speaks in the future tense, as if referring to life in Paradise. She herself later interpreted this text as being the design on earth for the Work which God had asked her to build. In an unpublished interview (April 21, 2002), she says: "We see our Work—our Movement—as a mystical rose." Here she describes it.

In our unity of "us"* and the focolarine, every now and then all the focolarine, will unite themselves to us to form, as it were, the bud of a mystical rose. Then they will distinguish themselves, detach themselves (in praise and repetition of the Trinity), as it were, into many petals, each of which will take the form of a rose, of a rosebud with other petals subdividing themselves, separating themselves out and forming in their turn other buds … The whole then will return to the heart bud. …

The rose then will open up in other ways, according to other relationships among the souls,

---

* It refers to the unity between Chiara and Igino Giordani, Foco and the patterns and the harmonies will be perennially new.

This transition, however, which implicitly contains detachment from game to game, from music to music, will be perfect joy: "Rejoice and be glad" (see Mt 5:12; Lk 6:23) because "Blessed are you when they separate you" (see Lk 6:22).

From a written passage, July 23, 1949

To be another Jesus

Before going to our brothers and sisters, we must be in unity with God. This is what St. Paul says: "If I speak ... but do not have love ..." (1 Cor 13:1) We must do nothing, not even lift a finger, or smile, if Jesus is not in us.

And we must do everything to the extent that Jesus wants to do it, no more, no less. That it be He alone, He completely, and He always, living in us.

Every moment of our life must have a wide dimension: as wide as God because we have to use all our strength to live it.

May everything always be consumed.

The soul in perfect unity with Jesus within it is *Alter Christus* [another Christ]. It realizes that it is another Jesus because his Presence imbues everything within it, and the soul also recognizes that it is another Jesus with Jesus within it, because it finds Him, whenever it desires, within itself.

We can reach this point by corresponding to grace, by being generous.

From a written passage, November 23, 1950

Chapter 4

How to contribute to unity

Unity is a gift of God, yet our personal commitment must be radical and constant. It is a commitment which comes from believing, praying, contemplating and, above all, from loving. All these attitudes give a precious contribution to the ecumenical journey toward the unity of the churches.

A personal, constant and radical commitment

We might ask ourselves: in a collective spirituality, completely committed to emphasizing communion, the community, how much personal commitment is required? How much individual effort?

We must respond: it requires at least as much as other spiritualities.

In fact, how can we love others if we have nothing or little of our own to offer?

And didn't Jesus say that for others we should sanctify ourselves …?

Personal commitment, for us too, therefore, must be constant and radical.

Rocca di Papa,
December 28, 1995[38]

1. Believe, Pray, Contemplate

Believing in Jesus present in unity

Chiara loved to cite—and she did it often—a verse from the First Letter of Peter: "Above all, maintain constant love for one another" (1 Pt 4:8). Often it was enough that she mentioned the first words: "above all," sometimes quoted in Latin — "ante omnia" — to make herself clear. When she is asked how to reconcile the life of mission and its necessary strategies with the life of unity, she answers that it's not a matter of reconciling but of prioritizing unity.

Brothers, Let everything else crumble — unity never! Where there is Unity, there is Jesus!

Put your three young hearts together and form a single Heart: the Heart of Jesus!

Be the real focolare of Assisi.

Always have this Fire burning among you.

And don't be afraid of dying. You've already experienced that Unity requires the death of everyone, to give life to the *One!*

With, or because of your death, *Life lives!*

The *Life* which, unbeknown to you, gives life to so many souls.

Jesus said so: "And for their sakes I sanctify myself, so that they also may be sanctified in truth" (Jn. 17:19).

To accomplish the Unity of all Assisi and the world, stay *united with each other.*

It's the only way.

That *Unity* in which Love dwells will give you strength to face every external disunity and to fill every void.

Do this as your sacrosanct *duty,* even though it brings you immense joy!

Jesus promised *the fullness of joy* to those who live Unity!

And don't be afraid of anything. Fear only that you might attach yourselves to something that is not *Jesus among you.* This is your and our Ideal.

Trent,
April 1, 1948[39]

Trust in the prayer of Jesus to the Father

You might say: but Chiara, the unity of the world is a utopia.

But who has said that it is a utopia? At a given moment, why can't the way people think change and take a new direction?

Why can't something change? If we put a wedge into the notion of unity, opening it up from here to there, and then the Almighty with us opens it from here to there? He is the one who rules history, who brings forward events, who is behind everything. So we go forward confident; the *ut omnes* is a reality for which Jesus prayed, and he is God who prayed to God. So God cannot say no to himself. Therefore, we go ahead with this confidence: we do our small part and he will do the big part.

Castel Gandolfo,
January 18, 1987[*]

To see in each person a candidate for unity

The Word "To the weak I became weak, so that I might win the weak. I have become all things

---

[*]   From a speech to the Gen (a term used for the second generation of the Focolare Movement) on occasion of the twentieth anniversary of their Movement's birth.

to all people, so that I might by any means save some" (1 Cor 9:22) … reminds us of the typical method of those who follow the way of unity so as to reach the *ut omnes* [that all may be one]: make ourselves one with every neighbor. Yes, this is the way because it is the very way chosen by God to show us his love. He became a human being like ourselves and was crucified and forsaken to put himself at everyone's level — truly weak with the weak. And thus he opened the way to the *ut omnes*. He bent down toward us; he was not broken. Just like the bamboo, used for so many things in the Philippines, because it bends but is not broken.

We are called to contribute to the fulfillment of the *ut omnes* and so, first of all, let's renew our faith that every person, every person is called to unity, since God loves everyone. Let's not make excuses, saying "that person will never understand"; "that one is too young"; "that's one of my relatives, I know him only too well, he is too attached to the things of this world"; "that one belongs to another religion"; "that person believes in spiritualism"; "this one is too old to change"; etc. Enough of these judgments! God loves everyone and is there waiting for them. The only thing we have to do is love each and every person, by serving them and by making ourselves completely one with them in everything but sin. Let Jesus worry about winning them over!

And he will; if not now, then in ten, or twenty, or thirty years. But he will! I know from experience.

Melbourne,
February 2, 1982[40]

Pray

Soon after the luminous reading of John 17, it became common practice for Chiara and her first companions, after receiving the Eucharist, to ask Jesus to use their lips to repeat that prayer to the Father every day. Chiara wrote to her companions in October 1947: "At Holy Communion in the morning, let Jesus raise HIS prayer to the Eternal Father.... Jesus obtains everything from the Eternal Father. Then offer your life 'ut omnes unum sint'—'So that they may all be ONE.'"[41] In November of the same year she wrote to Anna Melchiori: "Let Jesus pray when, alive, he lives in your heart after Holy Communion. Let him once again pray his final prayer to the Father that you may be made worthy to work for the greatest possible Ideal: God."[42]

The words of Scripture chosen this year by a large ecumenical group in the United States are taken from the first letter of St. Paul to the Thessalonians in Greece. It was a small, young community and Paul felt that the unity among them had to become more and more solid. That was why he urged them to "Be at peace among yourselves," to be patient with all, to not repay evil for evil, to always seek to do good to each another and to all, and also to "Pray without ceasing." He wanted to stress that the life of unity of the Christian community is possible only through a life of prayer. Jesus himself prayed to the Father for the unity of his disciples: "that they may all be one."

January 2008*

Contemplate the life of the Trinity

Jesus, on the cross and in his abandonment, really gave everything and emptied himself completely. And all this out of love for us. This was the measure of his love.

A measure that we too must learn to have with regards to our brothers and sisters: "Love one another as I have loved you," that is, to be totally empty of ourselves in order to welcome the sufferings and joys of others.

This is the love which is requested from us by God who is love.

Love, in fact, is not an attribute of God: it is his very Being, of Him who is one and three.

---

* From the Word of Life "Pray without ceasing" (1 Thess 5:17) on occasion of the Week of Prayer for Christian Unity.

The Father totally empties himself, so to speak, going out of himself, in a certain way becoming a "non-being" out of love, and generates the Son; and for this very reason, he is Father. The Son, in turn, as echo of the Father, out of love turns to the Father; and in a certain sense he too makes himself "non-being" out of love; and for this very reason, he is Son. The Holy Spirit, since he is the mutual love between the Father and the Son, their bond of unity, He too makes himself "non-being" out of love, that "non-being," that "emptiness of love" in which Father and Son meet each other and are one. And for this very reason he is Holy Spirit.

There are Three Persons in the Trinity, and yet they are One because at the same time Love is not and is, in an eternal self-giving.

This is the dynamism of life within the Trinity, which is manifested as unconditional reciprocal gift of self, mutually being nothing out of love, total and eternal communion.

A similar reality has been imprinted by God on the relationships among human persons. We had noticed it from the moment God first gave us his light. I too felt the same thing, years before, that I had been created as a gift for the person next to me and the person next to me had been created by God as a gift for me, just as the Father in the Trinity is everything for the Son and the Son is everything for the Father. And therefore, also the relationship among us can be the Holy Spirit, the same relationship that there is among the Persons of the Trinity.

It is the life of the Trinity that we can imitate, loving one another.

Therefore, life will no longer be lived only in the inner being of the single person, but it will freely become life of the entire human family.

September 7, 2003*

2. Love

We offer only a few texts concerning this point because much has already been published in this series on the art of loving or mutual love. Chiara indicated a few ways to maintain and make unity grow, describing the "instruments of the collective spirituality."

Service

The soul that desires to bring about Unity must keep itself at all times in an abyss of such humility that it reaches the point of losing, for the benefit and in the service of God in its neighbor, *its very self.*

It re-enters itself only to find God and to pray for its brothers and sisters and for itself.

---

* From a videotaped message to the meeting of Christian Associations of Italian Workers in Orvieto, Italy, entitled "Living hope in a global society of risk."

It must live constantly "emptied" because it is totally "in love" with God's will ... and in love with the will of its neighbor, who it wants to serve for God.

A servant does only what the Master commands.

If all people, or at least even a very small group of persons, were true servants of God in their "neighbor," soon the world would belong to Christ.

December 2, 1946[43]

Keeping alive the current of love and peace

Becoming one = feeling in ourselves the feelings of our brothers and sisters. Resolving their problems as though they were our own, made ours by charity. *Be the other person.* And do it out of love for God, for Jesus in our brother or sister.

Loosen the bonds of this hard, "stony" heart and have *a heart of flesh,* to love others.

"Let us love ... in truth and action" (1 Jn 3:18). Not, "Let's perform deeds and speak the truth." Instead, *let's love.* It is *loving* that counts.

And our *deeds* must have as their end, not the deed itself, but Jesus in our neighbor—*the neighbor* with whom we will be *one* out of love for Jesus.

Only Christ can make two into *one,* because his *Love,* which requires extinguishing self, the absence of egoism, allows us to reach the depths of another person's heart. Love. *I in you and you in me.*

Love our *neighbor* as ourselves. It is achieved only when the two are *one* and one becomes the other and the other becomes the former.

What matters is to keep alive and fired up this current of love and of peace which runs among us. Seek to make it penetrate ever more among all those who live around us.

December 12, 1946[44]

Knowing how to lose, how to give in

I would like to touch on a topic we have probably never touched on: my experience.

I am the president of the Movement; therefore, I could at times, perhaps, impose my ideas, and say, "But, no, things are like this!"

My experience is this: in order to have Jesus among us always, with serenity, with peace, and in order to bring ahead the Work of God, we have to know how to lose.

In other words, when someone tells you something, even if you feel that you have a thousand reasons, or a hundred reasons to prove that you are right, it is better to make yourself one with the idea of your brother or sister, unless it is a sin, because it is better to do what is less perfect, in unity, than to do what is more perfect by yourself.

And I see that, with the grace of God, I have learned this lesson, so that even if someone says to me, "Look, this is the way it is" and perhaps I know that it is not so, what does it matter, what does it matter! What matters is that there be Jesus among us, and even though I might be right, what does it matter?

I might ask, "Did you hear about such and such an event?" "Oh no, it wasn't like that at all, it was different." And I might have really heard the facts. In any case, if it is different, we'll hear about it.

So this is the point: to know how to lose, to know how to lose our own ideas, our own perspectives, our own convictions, in order to make ourselves one, as long as it is not sinful.

And then we must bring ahead the Movement with Jesus in our midst. If a particular truth has to come out, it will come out just the same. You can say it in another moment, it will come out just the same. Because, if you are determined to have Jesus in the midst, insisting on stating your opinion makes everything break down. A very great flexibility is needed.

I didn't just make a proposal; I made the decision to love, to see Jesus in everyone, as much as possible. But now, thinking about it in order to tell you what to do, I have noticed that knowing how to lose is the art of keeping Jesus among us, of not being stubborn about one's own ideas ... knowing how to lose and, naturally, if the other person accepts your opinion, you can offer it, but without [being attached to your own ideas].

This does not mean that we become passive and that nothing matters to us any longer. No, no, it's a passage, which keeps us from breaking unity, from causing a crack in unity. Then we go ahead and Jesus among us remains and is there in our midst.

Castel Gandolfo,
June 14, 1988[*]

Mercy and forgiveness

We had said we wanted to see only Jesus in our neighbor, to deal with Jesus in our neighbor, to love Jesus in our neighbor, but now we recall that a neighbor has this or that defect, has this or that imperfection.

Our eye becomes complicated and our being is no longer lit up. As a consequence, erring, we break unity.

Perhaps that particular neighbor, like all of us, has made mistakes, but how does God view him or her? What really is that person's condition, the truth of his or her state? If our neighbor is recon-

[*] From a speech to young men and women considering a life of consecration to God in the Focolare.

ciled with God, then God no longer remembers anything, he has wiped out everything with his blood. So, why should we go on remembering?

Who is in error in that moment?

I who judge or my neighbor?

I am.

Therefore I must make myself see things from God's viewpoint, in the truth, and treat my neighbor accordingly, so that if, by some mishap, he or she has not yet sorted things out with the Lord, the warmth of my love, which is Christ in me, will bring my neighbor to repentance, in the same way that the sun dries and heals many wounds.

Charity is preserved by truth, and truth is pure mercy with which we ought to be clothed from head to foot in order to be able to call ourselves Christians.

From a written passage,
sometime prior to 1959[45]

3. Becoming What We Are

The following written passages and excerpts from speeches emphasize the radical demands required from whoever wants to live unity.

There is no unity except where our personality* no longer exists.

*   Chiara does not intend the meaning of the word in a

We must not make a "mixture," but a "combination," and this will happen only when each personality loses itself in Unity, in the Heat of the Flame of Divine Love.

What remains of two or more souls that are combined? Jesus—the One.

No one gives as much glory to God as God, and God is in a soul which becomes nothing because Christ is re-living in it, and in Christ, the Father. And between two souls who fuse themselves (a mutual being-nothing out of love, the consequence of heroic humility and burning love) they give prominence to Christ.

When unity passes, it leaves only one trace: Christ.

A person who is fused in unity loses everything, but every loss is a gain.

Unity requires souls who are ready to lose their own personalities, their whole personality.

Because Unity is God, and God is *One and Three*.

The 3 live unifying themselves by their very nature which is Love, and unifying themselves (= making themselves nothing) they re-find themselves: 3->1->3. The 3 make themselves one out of

---

psychological sense but in terms of asceticism, along the lines of the gospel passage: "Those who find their life will lose it, and those who lose their life for my sake will find it" (Mt 10:39). See also next passage from the Diary of June 28, 1971.

love, and in the One Love, they rediscover themselves.

December 2, 1946[46]

It is Christ who lives in me

I received a book about St. [Peter Julian] Eymard. I transcribe a passage of it that has to do with the gift of one's own personality.

"At the end, I made the perpetual vow of my personality to Our Lord, Jesus Christ … asking for the grace that is essential to this gift: nothing for me; and taking as the model of this gift: the Incarnation of the Word.

"Just as in the mystery of the Incarnation, the sacred humanity of our Lord was made nothing in its own person, so that it no longer sought itself as an end, no longer had any interest of its own, no longer acted for its own sake, having in itself another person, that is, the Person of the Son of God, who sought only the interest of his Father …; so must I be made nothing to every desire of my own, to every interest of my own and have none but those of Jesus Christ, who is in me, in order to live in him for his Father. …

"It is as if my Savior said: In sending me on earth through the Incarnation, the Father has torn out of me every root of self-seeking, by not giving me the

human person, but uniting me to a divine person in order to make me live for him. In the same way, through Communion, you will live for me. . . .

"I shall be the person of your personality, and your personality will be the life of my person in you: 'It is no longer I who live, but it is Christ who lives in me' (Gal 2: 20)."

This is magnificent. So here we have a saint who confirms that we should not seek our own "personality," but lose it in Christ.

Jesus taught us this by making us understand that in unity with our brothers and sisters we lose our personality. That's how it is. I empty myself "to be the other"; or, in unity with God, I make myself empty to be the will of God for me.

On the other hand, it is precisely in this absolute "loss" that we acquire the fullest of personalities because Christ in me *loves* with my heart, thinks with my intellect (and so on) and everything which is *mine* is divinized by him and thus expanded to the infinite.

The saints are examples of the variety of personalities that Christianity, if lived deeply, can generate.

From the Diary, June 28, 1971[47]

Being fulfilled in unity

Q:—Chiara, we lived in Russia for seventy years with the idea of collectivism, seeking to build a Communist society. Now, many people think that unity suppresses the individual within the collectivity. How can I explain to them that the opposite is true, that unity leads to the full realization of the person?

It's because true unity is in the image of the Most Holy Trinity. We have only one God in three distinct Persons, and they are very different from one another: the Father is not the Son, the Son is not the Father, the Father and the Son are not the Holy Spirit.

Therefore, unity, true unity, that for which Jesus prayed, "May they be one as you and I" (see Jn 17: 21–22), enables you to fulfill yourself, the opposite of what one might think.

How can you accomplish unity? With love. The more you give, the more you are fulfilled, the more you are yourself because we have what we give; what we give makes us be. If we live unity we will be very different from one another, with very different personalities. And yet, we will all be one in Christ Jesus.

And so our nations, when they will be united, when the nation of the other is loved as one's own, they will have their own wonderful characteristics enhanced by unity and they will all be one, the great family of the children of God.

Rome,
May 20, 1995[48]

The Lord, enlightening us on the gospel, made us understand in a special way certain words of the gospel, especially those concerning love. So one word after another struck us like a flash of lightning, and these words eventually constituted the main lines—as Paul VI said—of a new spirituality: the spirituality of unity.

You will ask: what are they?

God-Love, but to love him, to do God's will. But which will of God? Loving. And if we love everyone, we love one another. But if we love one another, there is unity. And to have unity, Jesus crucified and forsaken: that is a mystery which has to be explained separately. But to have full unity: the Eucharist. And who is the image of unity, the mother of unity? Mary. What is the church? The church is organized unity, the church is love, said Paul VI in Sydney.[49] It's organized love, it's organized charity, communion. All these points that we took from the gospel formed our spirituality, which in practice could be presented as a medal, its thickness made up of all these words, on one side there is unity and on the other, Jesus forsaken....

Unity. In the end, when we live the whole of this spirituality, in a heroic way, in a full way, what emerges? What emerges — now I will tell you something very simple but very profound — is that we become what we are, as Augustine said. We already are another Christ, because we are baptized; we already are the body of Christ, because we have this bond among us and we are the body of Christ. We already are Christ, with Christ as the head and the body of Christ; we already are church, because we are baptized. Baptism does one part, but we must do the other part in order to be truly church, truly Christ individually, truly body of Christ.

The charism of unity helps Christians and the church, communities and groups to become what they are. We already are church, we already are Christ ... With this charism we become what we are.

Schoenstatt, Germany,
June 10, 1999*

---

* From a speech to the Schoenstatt Movement. Chiara reviews the various points of the spirituality in relation to unity, in order to later focus more on unity.

4. The Secret of Unity

The door that opens unity

Let's speak about unity. The mysterious word unity — as you know — appears in John's Gospel in the prayer (of Jesus) that is his Testament: "Father ... that they may all be one" (Jn 17:21). It asks for the unity of each man and woman with God and with one another.

Unity, however, is mysterious, in the way Jesus intends it, and certainly not easy to achieve. We need to know how to bring it about and to recompose it when it is broken. And so, this is why the Holy Spirit revealed the secret, the key. It is Jesus crucified who cries out: "My God, my God, why have you forsaken me?" (Mt 27:46). ...

He suffered this tremendous sense of division, of abandonment, of separation from the Father, precisely in order to reunite all people in God, separated as they were by sin, and to reunite human beings with one another. As you know, dear brothers and sisters, Jesus forsaken therefore has a lot to do with unity. And he has been defined as the "high road" to reach unity.[50]

In life, each of us has sufferings that are at least a little similar to his. Who does not feel, in some way, separated from God when a sense of darkness invades the soul? Who has not experienced doubts, perplexity, worries like Jesus who, on the cross, doubted, felt perplexed, asked "why?" Well then, when we feel anxiety, when we suffer, we should think of him, who made them his own. We should think of him, because these sufferings remind us of him, they are almost a presence of his, a countenance of his.

We should do as Jesus did, who was not petrified, blocked by the suffering, but added to that cry the words: "Father, into your hands I commend my spirit" (Lk 23:46), thus re-abandoning himself to the Father.

Like him we too must go beyond the suffering. ...

Also the small communities in which we live, the family, groups, the office, our centers, schools, and so forth, can experience small or significant divisions and make us suffer. There, too, we need to see Jesus forsaken and personally overcome that suffering in ourselves and do all we can to recompose unity with others. Likewise with regard to the larger realities, like those within our churches. We should work to recompose unity in them among the various individuals, associations, everywhere.

But love for Jesus forsaken also helps us to work towards the full unity among the various churches. Likewise, it is helpful in opening a dialogue with people of other religions, and also with those from other cultures which do not have any particular reference to religion. In short, Jesus forsaken can really be defined as the door that opens up unity.

Munich, Germany,
December 8, 2001[*]

To love Jesus Forsaken in the difficulties

Christ Crucified and Abandoned!

He is Everything!

If the world only knew Him!

If the souls that follow Unity only sought and welcomed Him as their only goal, as their All! Then Unity would never again suffer imbalances and breakdowns.

Try, Father, to embrace Him.

If I hadn't had Him in the trials of life, there wouldn't be Unity, unless Jesus desired to bring it about just the same somewhere else.

April 23, 1948[51]

Unity is only a vague dream without love for Jesus forsaken

Yesterday, when I learned that the Divine Will, the fatherly Hand of God had begun the salutary

[*] From a talk to evangelical ecclesial movements in Germany.

101

and necessary work of pruning the growing plant, I could hardly believe it. I was expecting it, but not so soon! And Jesus immediately made me see with how much predilection He loves you. He loves you. My little Brothers, if anything has taken up residence in your hearts that doesn't resemble joy for what is happening, then that heart must admit that it hasn't understood *Unity*.

What is happening to you is the logical consequence of the Ideal that we've proposed for ourselves.

It is *Jesus* who is among you who are united in His name. You form *Jesus*, and Jesus cannot but live life as Jesus does!

He said that the small tree that bore fruit would be pruned so that it might bear even better fruits. And so, aren't you rejoicing with the fullness of joy at seeing such care on the part of our Father for you?

Have you still not understood that the greatest Ideal the human heart could desire — Unity — is only a dream, a fantasy, if the one who wants it doesn't have as his only treasure in life *Jesus who was abandoned by all, even by His Father?* ...

It's only by *wholeheartedly* embracing Jesus Forsaken, all wounded in body and soul and covered by darkness, that our soul will be formed to *Unity*.

February 17, 1949[52] *

_____

* Chiara mentions a "pruning of the growing plant," but

Love the suffering caused by every disunity

In this month, to emphasize a concrete aspect of our love (for Jesus forsaken), let's love Him in the difficulties that unity among us entails.

We know it: unity … in our communities is not achieved once and for all. It must be rebuilt every day, and this is done by loving the suffering that non-perfect unity, always ready to occur, requires.

And this means to be always ready to see each other new; it means to be patient; to put up with others, knowing how to overlook flaws; it means to trust and to hope always, to believe always. Above all, it means not to judge. Merely human judgment towards others, especially those in a position of responsibility, is terrible: it's the opening through which the devil of disunity comes in. As a result, the good in our soul slowly fades away and the vocation itself may falter.

Let's look after this love for the others, full of painful nuances, which are the concrete aspect of our readiness to die for one another. There are small or big obstacles to overcome with our love for Jesus forsaken, so that unity may always be full. Then the Risen Lord will always live and shine forth throughout our Movement, throughout the

we don't know which "pruning" she refers to. A plausible theory is that of a ban at that time on having contact with members of the emerging Movement.

whole world, and He will guide it always forward toward the fulfillment of God's plan.

Rocca di Papa,
October 25, 1990[53]

We close this section on the relationship between Jesus forsaken and unity with a prayer from Chiara, which expresses the profound dynamic of her life. After having composed it, probably in 1957, she sang it to the tune of the well-known song "Auld Lang Syne," known in Italy as the "Waltz of the Candles."

Jesus, my heart awaits you at the end of life when I will go to love your love in Paradise.

Oh, how much I long for that moment, my Jesus, in which I will live forever in that peace that is you.

You know well, however, that my soul will only be satisfied when on earth all united will have entered into your heart.

And so grant me to suffer a little longer for unity so that humanity may be all one prayer to your heart.

From a prayer, 1957

5. How to Contribute to the Unity of the Churches

The ecumenical dialogue that Chiara promoted in the Focolare Movement she founded was not the result of an artificially created strategy, but was born out of circumstances, true signs of God's will, which she understood throughout her life. Sharing the spirituality of unity with people of various Christian churches creates a very strong bond, which made Chiara affirm at various moments: "No one will be able to separate us because it is Christ who binds us all together in what we call 'the dialogue of the people.'"

Spreading love and reciprocal love among the Churches

Love! What a great need there is for love in the world! And in us, Christians!

All together we Christians of various churches number more than a billion people. Such a multitude should be quite visible. But, unfortunately, we are so divided that many do not see us, nor do they see Jesus through us.

He said that the world would recognize us as his own and, through us, would recognize him, by our reciprocal love, by unity: "By this everyone will know that you are my disciples, if you have love for one another" (Jn 13:35).

Consequently, our uniform, our distinctive characteristic, was supposed to have been mutual love, unity. But we have not maintained full visible communion, nor do we have it now. Therefore, it is *our* conviction that also the Churches themselves must love one another with this love. And we strive to work in this direction.

How often the Churches seem to have forgotten the testament of Jesus, scandalizing the world with their divisions, while they should have been winning it over for him!

If we look at our 2,000 year history, and in particular at the history of the second millennium, we cannot help but see that it has often been a series of misunderstandings, of quarrels, of conflicts which in many places have torn the seamless tunic of Christ, which is his Church.

Certainly, this was caused by circumstances: historical, cultural, political, geographical, social. ... But it was also caused by the fact that among us there was a lack of this unifying characteristic of ours: love.

And so today, as we seek to make up for so much evil, to draw new strength for a fresh start, we must put all our confidence in this gospel love. ...

Our world today asks each one of us for love; it asks for unity, communion, solidarity.

And it also calls upon the churches to recompose the unity that has been lacerated for centuries.

This is the reform of all reforms which heaven is asking of us. It is the first and necessary step toward universal brotherhood with all men and women of the world. The world will believe if we are united. Jesus said so: "May they all be one ... so that the world may believe" (Jn 17:21).

God wants this! Believe me! And he repeats it and cries it out through the present-day circumstances he permits.

May he give us the grace, if not to see all this accomplished, at least to prepare for its coming.

Geneva, Switzerland,
October 27, 2002* 54

With the dialogue of life, a "Christian people" is composed

Now, after forty years of ecumenical life in the Movement, we can see emerging our specific contribution in the ecumenical field, based precisely on the spirituality of unity.

With brothers and sisters of the various churches, striving to live the gospel together, getting to know one another, reinforcing our reciprocal love, we

---

* The speech was delivered a few days before the celebrations for the anniversary of the Reformation, an event which involved all Lutheran and Reformed churches.

have discovered the great wealth of our common heritage: baptism, the Old and New Testaments, the dogmas of the first councils which we share, the creed (Nicene-Constantinopolitan), the Greek and Latin Fathers, the martyrs and other things, like the life of grace, faith, hope, charity, and the many other inner gifts of the Holy Spirit. And besides all this, we are united by the spirituality of unity.

Before this, we lived as if all this were not really true, or we were not fully aware of it. But now we realize they are the conditions for being able to achieve a particular dialogue: the dialogue of life.

Because of it we feel that we are already one family; we feel that we form among ourselves "a Christian people" which includes lay people, but also priests, pastors, bishops, and so on.

Obviously, the full and visible communion among our Churches still needs to be achieved, but we can already live this reality.

It is not a grassroots dialogue that runs contrary to or merely alongside that of official representatives or the church leaders, but a dialogue in which all Christians can participate.

This people is like leaven in the ecumenical movement that awakens in everyone the sense that, as baptized Christians capable of loving one another, we can all contribute toward realizing the Testament of Jesus.

Indeed, we hope that other forms of dialogue, like that of charity, of shared service, of prayer, the theological dialogue, can be empowered by the "dialogue of life."

Geneva, October 28, 2002 [55]

A prayer for unity among Churches

Jesus, here we are, those in charge of the World Council of Churches, bishops of various churches who adhere to the Focolare Movement, and leaders of the Focolare Movement itself. We have come together to get to know one another better, which we hope is in accordance with your will.

We are here first of all to ask you for something great, Lord!

You said: "Where two or three are gathered together in my name (in my love), there am I in the midst of them" (see Mt 18:20). Kindle in us all a great fraternal respect, help us to listen profoundly to one another, arouse among us that mutual love which allows, indeed ensures, your spiritual presence in our midst.

Because we know, Lord, that "without you we can do nothing" (see Jn 15:5).

But, with you in our midst, we will be given light by your light and be guided on this day when we will deal with an issue that touches us all and that concerns especially you and your Church.

You know the various tasks we have in it, or better, the one, yet varied, calling that weighs on each of us: to work, together with many others in the Christian world, so that full and visible communion among the churches may one day become a reality.

Even though this, we know, requires almost a miracle. This is why we need you, Jesus.

For our part, in this moment, before beginning such a demanding meeting, ever aware that we are "useless and unfaithful servants," we cannot help but open our hearts and reveal to you our deepest sentiments.

First of all, we feel the need to ask you for forgiveness on our own behalf, but also on behalf of our Christian brothers and sisters throughout the ages, forgiveness for having carelessly torn your tunic, for having cut it up into so many pieces, or for having kept it this way because of indifference.

At the same time, we cannot help but nurture a fervent hope in your mercy, which is always greater than any of our sins and capable not only of forgiving, but also of forgetting.

Just as we cannot deny that we have great faith in your immense love, which is able to draw good from every evil, if we believe in you and if we love you.

All this burns in our hearts, Jesus, in this moment, together with gratitude for what Christians of many Churches have been able to do, with your grace, for almost a century. Prompted by the Holy Spirit, they have worked toward mutual reconciliation through a fruitful dialogue of love, intense theological work, and a general raising of people's awareness of the need for unity.

And so, allow us to tell you, Lord, that although we are still in the acutely painful situation of not yet having achieved full communion, we sense in our hearts the Christian optimism that your infinite Love cannot but help kindle.

We begin our work, then, confident that you, who know how to conquer the world, will help us to help you fulfill your testament here on earth one day. Then, with unity achieved, your testament will witness to the world that you are the King and Lord of all hearts and peoples. Amen.

Geneva, October 28, 2002* [56]

---

* Before delivering the speech of which we have presented a passage above, Chiara had been invited by Dr. Konrad Raiser, secretary general at the time of the WCC, to express a prayer.

Chapter 5

Universal brotherhood and a united world

Certain words, which originated in the gospel, have spanned history. Two of these are unity and fraternity [also known as "universal brotherhood"]. The two terms recall each other even though they are distinct, and as such they appear from the very beginning in the story of Chiara and the spirituality linked to her name. As Chiara explained in the preceding pages, unity refers to God and to Jesus who asks for it to the Father on our behalf. And as such, it characterizes the lifestyle which Christians should have.

The term "brotherhood" accentuates the relationship among people, who having in common a heavenly Father, are brothers and sisters to each other. In Western culture, the term has been gradually "secularized" to the point that, instead of the word "unity," Chiara can use it in the dialogue between believers and non-religious people of different cultures, in order to make a journey "together" toward unity. Not only: the word "brotherhood" is also a sure foundation in a dialogue based on the so-called "golden rule" ("Do unto others as you would have them do to you") among Christians and believers of the great world religions and of the traditional religions on various continents. As Chiara reminds us, the "golden rule" is present in nearly all the religious traditions of the world.

Because of the closeness and mutual reference to the meanings and realities contained in the two words unity and brotherhood, it seems necessary that we dedicate a section of this book to texts of Chiara related to brotherhood.

Then there is an "original" expression in Chiara's thought, which she uses frequently, especially with regards to the younger generations (youth and teenagers): "united world." She proposes it to those who represent today's world as it opens up to the future as the objective, the goal, the ultimate horizon within which to place one's own action and life. The "united world" thus becomes a creative synonym for unity and "universal brotherhood."

What is our vocation: Unity or universal brotherhood?

When we speak of unity we usually think of Christians. In fact, all the scripture scholars agree that when Jesus said "may they all be one," he meant for his disciples to be one with the Most Holy Trinity. They had the grace of God and they could be one.... Instead, we speak of universal brotherhood when we go also outside of Christianity and try to love everyone, to build a relationship, based on the "golden rule" perhaps, with many [faithful of other religions or people of no religious beliefs].

What is it that we have? We have both of these realities. In the early days, unity came into greater evidence. For some time now, perhaps during the past ten years, brotherhood emerged more forcefully because this is the way God does things: one step at a time. He knows everything but he instructs us a little at a time.

It made me very happy during these days to find a copy of what might be the very first talk I gave when we were still in Trent, in the Massaia Hall.* This first set of notes says: "The soul must, above all else, keep the gaze fixed on the one Father of many children. Then look at all creatures

---

* In the 1940s, Chiara held morning meditations at a hall located next to the church of San Marco, in the city center of Trent.

as children of the one Father. With thoughts and with the affections of the heart, always go beyond every limit imposed by human life, and tend constantly, and because of an acquired habit, toward universal brotherhood." So from the moment we were born we had brotherhood in our heart. Then God cultivated unity in us and, for some time now, also brotherhood. So our ideal is unity and universal brotherhood.

Madrid, December 8, 2002[*]

Understanding and spreading the spirit of brotherhood

Q:—How can we make the concept of brotherhood more understandable? This is a question that torments me. How can we convey our ideas without emphasizing concepts which are too generic?

I will try to respond one question at the time. So, what do we mean ... by brotherhood? It is that reality in which all men and women feel like brothers and sisters because they are all children of only one Father. Certainly, for us Christians this concept is a bit special because it coincides with

---

[*] From a moment of dialogue with a large group of people from Spain, from a variety of social and cultural backgrounds and ecclesial commitments, all of whom are active in living out and spreading the spirituality of unity.

the unity asked for by Jesus in his testament: "may they all be one." Unity, so to speak, is the "super" brotherhood, because it's unity in God through Jesus Christ in the Holy Spirit; it's unity in God. Since we are children of God, we are "one" in a special way; we have a Christian brotherhood that is a little bit characteristic of us, and generally is not possible outside of Christianity. . . .

We, Christians, with our supernatural love, loving [those who are not Christians] and being loved by them with the love they have within, and that we must help develop, by making them aware they have it, this is how we create brotherhood in the whole world. . . .

Something else: How can we be understood by the man or woman in the street? I would like to say something now that may appear new: by starting to live it out ourselves. If we put brotherhood into practice, we will have life experiences. For example, I meet a Muslim person, we talk, become friends. . . . Instead of talking about brotherhood, I should start by sharing my experiences, but it's necessary that I live it [so that] I can offer it. A life experience is never too difficult to understand, we can always offer it, it's enough to explain it well, it's enough to love and use words that everyone understands.

So my answer is: in order to be understood by the person in the street, we must start to live out this brotherhood, with everyone, and share our experiences.

Baar, Switzerland,
November 16, 2001*

For the "gestation of a new world"

We should look ahead without ever losing sight of the project that God seems to have for the world.

He, the Creator, is the Father of his creation and we, men and women from all over the earth, are his sons and daughters, all members of the one human family. The history of humanity is a slow and labored rediscovery of this universal brotherhood.

After millennia in which we have experienced the consequences of violence and hatred, we have every right today to ask that humanity begin to experience the consequences that love can have. And not only the consequences of love among individuals, but also among peoples.

God made humankind in his image, in the image of the Trinity, not only as individuals, but as society.

---

* From a moment of dialogue with bishops of various Churches gathered to examine in depth the life and doctrine of the spirituality of unity.

It was on man and woman together that God placed the imprint of the Trinity. And he intends the same design of communion for all humanity.

Consequently, the nations are also called to love one another, not to ignore one another or fight with each other.

Mutual love must become the law not only of relationships among individuals but also among communities. To love other countries as we love our own must become a reality.

If it is a right that every nation cultivates its own identity and develops its own spiritual and material gifts, they should know that these gifts will be perfected and enhanced by putting them at the service of other nations, in respect and mutual exchange.

Then yes, we can rightly dream (if we, along with everyone else, will do our part) as did Paul VI when he foresaw the world one day guided by a world authority. We will be able to dream that the Lord is leading the world toward a "new" order, to the point of forming one global community.

This is not a dream or a utopia if God is present and works with us for world unity.

Indeed, it would not be a bad idea for us to take the responsibility from now on to spread this concept by speaking about it, by writing about it, by communicating it with every means at our disposal.

119

We should present this project to government leaders, to intellectuals, to people in the social and cultural fields of every kind and at all levels. We should make it available to educators, young people, men and women of the entire world so that all people may search the depths of their heart and ask what personal contribution they can give. No one should feel excluded from this "gestation of a new world." Every person in his or her large or small world of daily activities — in the family, office, factory, labor union, immersed as they may be in local and general problems, in public institutions of the city or beyond, all the way to the United Nations — can truly be a builder of peace, a witness to love, an instrument of unity.

As far as we are concerned, let us walk as the children of Israel walked behind Moses. Let us walk behind Jesus who is among us. He will accomplish his plans as he has done thus far, never abandoning us. One day he will show us the promised land: a world that is united and in peace, for his glory and for the good of humanity.

Castel Gandolfo,
June 11, 1988[57]

Living for a united world

Q:—Very many young people can only see things negatively. They don't see that the situation is changing both in the political field as well as in the ecological and religious fields. They don't understand our motto: "To live for a united world." They think it is an illusion. Nor can we ourselves imagine really well how a united world will be. Will it be paradise on earth or just all the nations united? Could you give us your vision of a united world?

Always assuming that God wants it, we cannot see in detail how a united world will be … nor can we see when this united world will come about. But some things are sure. First of all, we are convinced that Jesus wants it because he said to his apostles, "Go into all the world and proclaim the good news." Therefore, everyone is a candidate to unity, to the gospel, to a united world — all are candidates. And Jesus said, "may they all be one," which means: all. So the first thing we can be sure of is that Jesus wants it.

Secondly, we know for sure that Jesus prayed for unity. Since the Son of God prayed to the Father for this, I think it will have to be granted, because it is impossible for the prayer of the Son of God not to be granted.

Another thing that we members of the Movement are sure of is that this charism was purposely sent by God for the unity of the world. It is remarkable how our Movement has spread to every nation, even to the smallest islands, where you can also find someone of the Movement. And it is not we who did it. It was God who spread the Movement in this way. It is like a network which enables you to see that God has a plan for the world. So there is this charism, and God doesn't send it for nothing. He has his purposes. And this is our third conviction.

Then another thing we can be sure of is this: we can see many things evolving. On the religious level there is the unity of the churches, for example. In the past this couldn't even be mentioned. On the political level, look at Europe; look at the social and ecological fields, and so on. It seems that all this evolution, although surrounded by numerous contradictions, is creating a "cradle," just like in the Roman Empire, which allowed Christianity to spread and reach beyond all boundaries.

This tendency which is evolving in the world could certainly be, in the plan of God, a preparation for a greater spreading of Christianity and therefore also of the ideal of a united world. These are our convictions.

Of course, we cannot convince young people that the world will be united, because it's a supernatural idea, not something human. As a matter of fact, we shouldn't talk about it too much. It is much better to get young people to come to our activities, where there are people of all races and also of different religions and Christian denominations. And what happens, for example, in our small towns, in our Gen-Fests or other events, is that young people share their impressions, saying: "I have understood. The united world is not a utopia. It can happen. I thought it was impossible, but if it has been achieved here among one or two thousand people, why can't it be achieved with everyone?" They begin to have faith in a united world, and then they become apostles for a united world.

Augsburg,
November 26, 1988*

Do not be afraid to speak of unity

Q:—Due to our experience with Communism, some words like "brotherhood" and unity have lost their true meaning. In fact, they sometimes have a negative connotation. How can we express the beauty of true unity founded on God?

---

* From a dialogue with a large group of people from Germany of different ages, social and cultural backgrounds and ecclesial commitments, who are personally committed to live and spread the spirituality of unity.

Your problem is similar to the one we had at the beginning of the Movement. At that time, in fact, no one used the word unity in Italy, only the Communists. Likewise, the word "love" was used only in the worst sense of the word. Also the word "brotherhood" was used only in certain environments. But we went ahead just the same because we were convinced that our unity would last because it was based on God.

We didn't give any thought to that "other" kind of unity; we knew that our unity would last.

And the same applies to the word "brotherhood," it would last, because ... [Jesus] said that we should all be brothers and sisters. "You are all brothers." So we went ahead, and I really feel that we have won, because the other unity has faded a little. The word unity is very beautiful, it's beautiful also for those who use it as a simple word, but the meaning that we give to it is better, we think, and it has survived.

With regard to the word "brotherhood" — we're building this brotherhood all over the world, not only with Catholics, but with all other Christians, with members of other religions, like the Muslims, for example, and also with people of good will who are very capable and to whom we are very grateful.... This brotherhood is a lasting one and it continues to spread.

So don't worry about this. Go ahead. Continue to speak of unity. If someone really can't understand what you mean, you can say: "The unity Jesus intended." And if someone really doesn't understand what you mean by brotherhood, say: "Jesus said that we should all be brothers and sisters." Add an explanation, out of charity, but be courageous and go ahead without worrying about anything.

Zagreb (Croatia),
April 18, 1999*

---

* From a dialogue with a large group of people (from Croatia, Slovenia, Bulgaria, Romania, Bosnia-Herzegovina, and Macedonia) of different social and cultural backgrounds and ecclesial commitments, personally involved in living to live and spread the spirituality of unity in nations formerly under Communist rule.

Spread a powerful current of brotherhood

In this context then, to work precisely for the unity of peoples, respecting their many different identities, is the best thing we can do and is the very purpose of politics, the greatest common good we can hope to attain.

But what is the method, the way to reach this goal?

There is no better way to reach such a high and demanding goal than to spread throughout the world a powerful current of brotherhood. It is the essential gift that Jesus gave to humanity. Shortly before dying, he prayed: "Father ... that they may all be one" (see Jn 17:11–21), and in revealing the fatherhood of God, he introduced to humanity the idea of universal brotherhood.

November 18, 2003,
delivered on November 28, 2003*

---

* From a videotaped message to politicians of Brasilia.

Unity: the medicine for today's world

Q:—At the birth of the Gen Movement you handed over to us a program of life: "It will be the cry of Jesus forsaken, which will re-echo to the very ends of the earth. And in that cry the whole world will hope again." We, Gen of the year 2000, feel this program to be our own. What can you tell us from your experience so that this program may be fully realized?

[Why did I say] to bring the cry of Jesus forsaken to the very ends of the earth? Because Jesus forsaken is the medicine, the medicine, one of the strongest medicines for the needs of today's world. . . .

In our times, while I am still here, we can see that this medicine of unity is already being requested. I remember something that happened when we were young, your age. There was a convent near Trent where the sisters argued a little with one another. I was very young, but they called me to speak to these sisters, to preach my Ideal in order to bring them together, to bring unity there. Even then people understood that there was a medicine in the charism of unity for the internal disunity they were experiencing.

Also recently, two years ago, as you know, I went to Graz in Austria where there was a large-scale ecumenical meeting, and they asked me to speak. I spoke of our Movement, of the points of our spirituality: of God-Love, the will of God, unity, Jesus in the midst, Jesus forsaken.... What emerged? Well, the great majority said: "This is an ecumenical spirituality! This serves to build unity among the churches; it serves to build unity among Christians!"

I just returned from Amman [Jordan]. There, instead, I participated in an interreligious conference at which there were representatives of many religions. The secretary general [of the symposium] said to me: "Chiara, speak at the end of the conference, because in your talk there is something that can be of service to all religions." I wondered: but I'm a Christian, I'm a Catholic, I have my own very clear truth, how can it be useful to all religions? And then I understood: it's because in all religions there are the "seeds of the Word," there is something of the Truth.... When Jesus redeemed us, he gave us the whole truth, but he also sent a little bit of truth here and there, here and there, he [distributed it].

For example, you know the famous "golden rule" that says: "Do to others what you would have them do to you. Do not do to others what you would not have them do to you." It's a seed of the Word. The Word is the Word of God, a small seed is thrown there. Where? In all religions. Almost all religions have this principle.

So I said: they asked me to give the final address because the others are able to relate to our way of presenting Christianity. ... At that convention we saw that disunity among religions, at times struggles, even wars among religions (you know history, also current events: fundamentalists in many parts of the world are fighting against other religions), can, through our Ideal, which is this charism, this medicine for unity, find positive solutions, and religions can come together, at least on the basis of some common principles, fundamental principles, because love is fundamental for all of us. ...

People are beginning to see that the charism of unity is really a charism that serves to bring unity. But in the future, when you will be older, they'll ask for you to go everywhere: there's disunity between the generations; there's disunity between husband and wife; disunity in groups; disunity between movements, disunity between nations, disunity between languages. ... They'll call you everywhere and this medicine will become a universal legacy.

And in this way we will contribute towards what? Towards a united world. This is the way we will build a united world, by earnestly, seriously uniting it through our charism of unity.

This morning I read something that three Popes, Pius XII, John XXIII and Paul VI, said: that the day will come in which the world will be so united that there will be only one authority, one political, social authority.

In the meantime, let's bring things ahead: perhaps the gen 3* will see this epoch of only one authority. In the meantime, let's go ahead towards a united world with our charism, the charism of unity, which is a universal medicine.

Castel Gandolfo, December 20, 1999[†]

Unity and universality

We found appealing the fact that unity — as we noted from Jesus' prayer — could not be disconnected from universality, because it says, "that they may all be one!"

"If this Ideal had come on earth," as we wrote [in 1960], "during the time of St. Francis, for example, it would not have been achievable because America had not yet been discovered.

"In this century, instead, unity is possible. Since we were born in the era of airplanes, radio, and television, we are more likely to reach unity, if we always aim high. And it will come about in a natural way, certainly not in our generation, and

---

* Teenagers in the Movement who are committed to live for unity.
† From a dialogue with young people of the Gen Movement (New Generation) committed to witness and spread the spirit of unity.

perhaps not even in the next or the one after that, but little by little it will, yes, all over the world."

Here is another thought from those years with regard to the universality of our Ideal of unity:

"Jesus' Testament does not only say, 'May they be one as you are in me and I am in you', but it says 'May they *all* be one.'

"Our focolares, our Movement would be a closed circle if we did not have universality as well as unity. If the stamp of universality does not go hand in hand with our unity, our unity is false.

"Our religious community is the world. We must, certainly, come together in community, gather with one another ('ecclesiastical' comes from *assembly, to gather together*), but ... in order to gather together everyone."

September 21, 2002[58]

Chapter 6

The "rainbow" as expression
of the life of unity

After almost a decade of strong illuminations regarding the mystery of God and God's
design for humanity that culminated in the
"Paradise" of the summer of 1949, the spirituality of unity, which Chiara was experiencing
and spreading, seemed to be complete. But
God was holding another surprise: in 1954, he
made her understand that this love that held
together a growing number of people had an
order, a "structure" which was articulated
in the "seven colors" of the rainbow. Seven,
a symbolic number, indicates the countless
ways in which the love of God, which is unity,
can be expressed in human life and in history.

The life of unity, which has its origin and
model in God, responds fully to the demands
of human life, which is characterized by the
three dimensions of the person: the spiritual,
the psychological and the physical-biological.
The relational nature of the human being is
inscribed in these three dimensions and is
very well expressed in the seven aspects or

colors, in which the fundamental relationship with God, with ourselves and with the others is enshrined and actualized.

In the following years, the experience of Chiara and the thousands of people around the world involved in the "divine adventure" of unity proved that this "seven-color" lifestyle could be applied in the most varied sectors of society as well.

Why, in this brief anthology of annotated texts of Chiara on unity, do we include a reference to the theory and life of the "colors"? Because it seems that it has a close and inseparable relationship with the subject of unity, inasmuch as we cannot aim at the fulfillment of this "dream" of God concerning humanity without, at least to some degree or in some way, "ordering" our own personal and social life according to this model and style of relationships. From this viewpoint, it is safe to say that, in a certain sense and even though in different ways, conforming our own existence to these seven aspects is a "way" that is good for everyone.

Initial intuitions

We are like a living Mass, a living Host, a living Eucharist, truly that Jesus who comes inside us in the morning, exactly as he is, perfectly visible in us through the transparency of our nothingness.

Visible, just as we see the seven colors through a drop of water or a lens or a glass; we: one of the seven (infinite colors) = a member of the Mystical Body that at the same time (and because of the Trinitarian law) is Jesus himself. But if it weren't for the lens (that is, the free soul as God created it) there wouldn't be the rainbow. God cannot show himself to the world ... as He is — in perfect Light — except in the Unity of all of us, and in each one of us, if we are united to the others.

From a written passage, Fregene,
October 15, 1949

1. The "Colors" – the Life of Unity Considered from Different, Interconnected Perspectives

Through the charism of unity, the Lord wished to bring about in the church not only a spirituality but also a society, which later was given the name Focolare Movement or Work of Mary.

Undoubtedly, this "Work" needs to have a soul (precisely what our communitarian spirituality is), but it also needs to have an order, a structure. And the Lord took care of this, too.

If I remember correctly, it was in 1954. The spirituality seemed to be more or less complete. And one thing had become clear to us: we had to become another Jesus. ...

But how could we accomplish this? Baptism and the other sacraments had certainly already made us such, but our adherence was necessary as well, and this could be summarized in one word: love. Love sums up the Christian law. If we love, we are another Jesus. And we are Jesus in all that we do. Our life, therefore, had to be love. If we had wanted to describe what we should be, we would have had to say, "We are love," just as God is love. And if love was our life, love had to be our rule as well.

And that's when the idea came, perhaps an illumination.

Love is light, it is like a ray of light that passes through a drop of water and opens out to display a rainbow, whose seven colors we admire; they are all colors of light, which in turn expand into an infinite number of shades.

And just as the rainbow is red, orange, yellow, green, blue, indigo and violet, love, the life of Jesus in us, is manifested in different colors; it is expressed in various ways, each one different from the others.

Love, for example, leads to communion, it is communion. Jesus in us, because he is love, brings about communion.

Love is not closed within itself but by its nature it spreads. Jesus in us, Love, reaches out to others in love.

Love elevates the soul. Jesus in us raises our souls to God. This is union with God, this is prayer.

Love heals. Jesus, Love in our hearts, is the health of our souls.

Love gathers people together in assembly. Jesus in us, because he is Love, joins hearts together.

Love is the source of wisdom. Jesus in us, Love, enlightens us.

Love gathers many into one, this is unity. Jesus in us fuses us into one.

These are the seven main expressions of love we had to live, and they represent an infinite number of expressions.

These seven expressions of love immediately appeared to us as the standard for our personal life, and they would also constitute the Rule of the Work of Mary as a whole, and later on of its various branches.

Because love is the principle of each of the above expressions, of each aspect (since it is always Jesus who lives in us in every aspect of life), our life would be marked by a wonderful unity.

Everything was to flow from love, be rooted in love; everything was to be an expression of the life of Jesus in us. And this would make human life attractive, fascinating. Consequently, our lives would not be dull and flat since they would not be made up of bits juxtaposed and disconnected (with the time for lunch, for example, having nothing to do with the moment for prayer, and with mission set aside only for a specific hour, and so on).

No. Now it would always be Jesus who prayed, Jesus who engaged in mission, Jesus who worked, Jesus who ate, Jesus who rested, and so on. Everything would be an expression of him.

Castel Gandolfo,
February 15, 1998[59]

Each aspect is considered in its root, which is in God, who, since He is Love, is Trinity, and also in its "incarnated" content in our life. Each aspect, lived in love, is an expression of the life of unity and in unity, and contributes to increasing the unity among all.[*]

The 7 aspects regard our life as a Mystical Body, considered from different perspectives:

The first highlights the communion among the different members, as the effect of evangelical love, and it is modeled after the *Communion of Saints*, which includes Jesus and Mary,

The second contemplates spreading [the Gospel] that a life as a Mystical Body entails: "*that they may all be one* … so that the world may believe" (see Jn 17:21).

---

[*] Italics added by the editor.

The third refers to the perfect *union with God* and with our neighbors that a spirituality lived as a Mystical Body produces (in mutual love there is perfection, holiness).

The fourth focuses on *what binds the members of the Mystical Body*, like a divine knot: "Jesus in the midst," the spiritual health of the Body, which refers also to every other form of health.

The fifth speaks of the integration of one member into another, *their harmony*, their life together, modeled on the Most Holy Trinity which makes them church, assembly, society, and also refers to every church building, every house, every attire used by a person or persons.

The sixth has to do with *the One who circulates among the members of the Mystical Body*, the Holy Spirit, who is expressed in Wisdom, in light, and requires studying.

The seventh expresses *that unity among the different members* ["We, who are many, are one body" (see Rm 12:50)] which is achieved on earth through full spiritual communication, and by using all the means of communication that are available.

Mollens, Switzerland,
June 30, 1999[60]

2. A look at the individual colors

Communion of goods (red)

From the earliest days of the Focolare, looking at our model, Jesus crucified and forsaken ... we understood that faithfulness to mutual love would bring about unity according to the life of the Trinity.... "It is the life of the Most Holy Trinity that we must try to imitate by loving one another ... as the Persons of the Most Holy Trinity love one another."

And the dynamism of the life within the Trinity is the unconditional mutual gift of Self; it is total and eternal communion ("All that is mine is yours, and all that is yours is mine," Jn. 17:10) between the Father and the Son in the Spirit.

Rocca di Papa,
November 5, 1995[61]

We have to keep in mind the way the Acts of the Apostles presents the life of the early Christians: "Now the whole group of those who believed were of one heart and soul, and no one claimed private ownership of any possessions, but *everything they owned was held in common....* There was not a needy person among them, for as many as owned lands or houses sold them and brought the proceeds of what was sold. They laid it at the apostles' feet, and it was distributed to each as any had need." (Acts, 4:32–35)

A first consideration that we can make concerning such a step is that unity of heart and unity of soul, fruit of mutual love, have as an immediate consequence *the communion of material goods.*[62]

Castel Gandolfo,
December 5, 1997[*]

In the Movement we live the communion of goods. We know, of course, that others in the church have lived and continue to live such communion, but for the most part they were, and still are, selected groups of persons, those with a special calling, such as monks and nuns in monasteries and convents.

In the Movement, it is the *whole of society* that lives the communion of goods, including lay people, as it was among the first Christians. To reach this goal, we seek to mirror the communion of saints and we live according to the model of the Trinity, where it is true to say *Omnia mea tua sunt*, "All that is mine is yours" (see Jn 17:10)....

The newness of this aspect lies in the way we deal with our goods and money. Usually, we do not

---

[*] From a speech to members who are consecrated in the Focolare in order to spread the spirit of unity.

give away our possessions (as the focolarini do) or our surplus (like others do) as separate individuals, but *we decide together what to give, and we put it in common.*

Rocca di Papa,
December 6, 1970[63]

Witness and outreach (orange)

As I was walking along the streets of Einsiedeln, in Switzerland, I saw many people of various religious orders passing by. The different habits of the sisters and priests were very beautiful against the background of such a splendid natural setting. I understood there that the founders were really inspired in dressing their followers in that particular way.

[Among these], I was particularly impressed by Charles de Foucauld's Little Sisters of Jesus. They rode by on their bicycles, their faces full of life and with simple scarves on their heads. Their expressive faces reminded me of their founder, de Foucauld, who, they say, cried out the gospel just by the way he lived.

In fact, those sisters seemed to say: "Blessed are the poor in spirit, blessed are they who mourn, blessed …"

These are not the beatitudes that the world would like to have, but rather the scandal of the gospel.

Then, I too felt a great desire to be able to give my witness, also in an external way.

(But) ... no solution came to me.

At a certain point I said to one of my companions: "You know ... I saw how those sisters had an effect on me, not through their words but by the way they dressed." ... I said I wished we could do the same. But how can *we* tell people about God? "Oh," I said, "By this everyone will know that you are my disciples, if you have love for one another" (Jn 13:35).

Mutual love, therefore, was to be our distinctive sign. Dying to ourselves in mutual love is our typical apostolic activity.

December 25, 1962[64]

Spirituality and prayer life (yellow)

Q: — I think that the spiritual way that the members of the Movement follow is defined as a collective, communitarian way. Is that true? And if so, could you tell us a little about the way of unity as a collective way?

Ours, precisely because it is a "way of unity," is a "collective way."

In fact, if we compare our way to others proposed by existing spiritualities in the church, we can notice how in the others, the emphasis is put more on the individual aspect, even though all the spiritualities in the Church of Christ, brought about by a genuine charism, do not, nor could ever be, only individual. You cannot be a Christian and not emphasize love which, to some degree, always makes us progress together. Furthermore, the mystery of the Mystical Body does not allow us to conceive, in our religion, of a solely individual spiritual way. Since we are members of a body, the negative or positive actions of a member have an influence on the whole body. . . .

Ours, in fact, is a way in which we go to God through our neighbor. I—my neighbor—God was the three-fold expression used by Igino Giordani to describe our way. We go to God through the human being; or better, we go to God with human beings, with our brothers and sisters. It is a way, therefore, which is distinctly collective. And in this collective way, each individual finds his or her own personal perfection.

In other spiritualities, those who seek God within themselves are like persons in a garden with many flowers, but look at and admire just one flower. They admire, love and adore God within themselves.

Instead, it seems to us that God is asking us to look at many flowers because the Lord is present in the others as well, or he can be.

And just as I must love God within myself — when I am alone — so I must love him in my brothers and sisters when I am with them.

Thus I will not love so much the flight from the world, but the search for Christ in the world. I will not only love solitude, but also companionship, not only silence but the spoken word as well.

And when this love towards Christ in our neighbor is mutual, in our encounter we live according to the model of the Trinity, where the two persons relate to one another like the Father and the Son, and between them bursts forth the Holy Spirit with his gifts, the soul of the Mystical Body. When Jesus is the reason for the encounter between brothers and sisters, they become one as God is one, but they are not alone, just as God is not alone, although he is one, because God is Love.

February 10, 1984*

Q: — It's not always easy to speak with God. What can we do to find an immediate relationship with God?

---

* From a dialogue with Catholic bishops who want to examine in depth the life and doctrine of the spirituality of unity.

There is a way to reach union with God which is quite fast and typical of our spirituality.

If you know how to have an authentic dialogue with your brothers and sisters, if you enter into your neighbor, if you welcome your neighbor truly and completely into yourself, with all of his or her problems and ideas, and if you love so much that you are accepted by the other person, you are practically living with your neighbor according to the model of the Most Holy Trinity. This method which has been experienced [by many] is the fastest way to reach union with God and a conversation with him.

The dialogue with your brother or sister leads you to union with God.

When you do this all day long, and in the evening you pause for prayer, you feel that the dialogue with God has begun, heaven opens up, something seems to have opened up wide, so that you can speak with God.

Grächen, Switzerland,
July 21, 1995[65]

Nature and physical life (green)

This is how we consider the aspect to which we have given the name *Agape.*

Why? Because *Agape* means Love, but a love that binds us together. It is not just any kind of love, but a love that binds ... The Mystical Body seen not in individual members, but in He who binds them together.

Vigo di Fassa,
August 19, 1955[66]

[The Mystical Body of Christ] is composed of all Christians bound to one another by mutual love, and to Christ, their head. The vitality of the Mystical Body lies precisely in the unity of all its members who, like the first Christians, are one heart and one soul. Just as whenever there is some ailment in the bodily organs, there is no health, likewise when there is no harmony among Christians, there is no "health" in the Mystical Body.

Rocca di Papa,
June 25, 1968[67]

The Communion of Saints, the Mystical Body exists. But this Body is like a network of darkened tunnels.

The power to illuminate them exists; in many individuals there is the life of grace, but Jesus did not want only this when he turned to the Father, calling upon him. He wanted heaven on earth: the unity of all with God and with one another; the network of tunnels to be illuminated; the presence of Jesus to be in every relationship with others, as well as in the soul of each.

As the sun cannot but warm up, so love cannot but renew and reinvigorate each member and group of the Mystical Body, the Church.

From a written passage,
sometime prior to 1959[68]

Psychologically speaking, it is impossible for individuals "to have a sense of identity" if there are not others who recognize them as subject.

Psychologists of all schools agree that human beings need to reaffirm one another in their individuality through genuine interactions and contacts.

In fact, in order to be able to be a gift for the others, first one must feel and be recognized as being "different" from the others.

But in order to be a personal gift it is necessary to enter into communion with others.

And herein lies the difference between so-called "interest groups" and the Christian community as Jesus intended. An interest group is composed of individuals who come together with a particular goal in mind (athletic clubs, civic, political or religious associations, trade unions, schools, study groups ...) and whose interaction is limited to carrying out those common interests. As for all that falls outside the realm of such common interests, these individuals remain closed in on themselves.

The Christian community, instead, is not formed for reasons that are external to the nature of community, but as a result of the very character of love which creates communion.

And experience confirms that this type of community is possible. It is clear that the motivation to bring about such a community comes from Jesus' invitation: "Love one another as I have loved you ... that they may all be one" (see Jn 15:12; 17:21). Obviously, this is religious in nature. But the psychological effects are extraordinary: each one, being a relationship of love with others, as a consequence becomes fulfilled as an authentic person.

Malta, February 26, 1999[69]

Harmony and surroundings (blue)

Here, too, as in the rest of our life, what must guide us is love. Also for what concerns our surroundings we should be guided by love, which leads us to make ourselves one with others. So ours will not be a poor house, or a rich one: we can live in a palace or a slum, in a skyscraper, in a country cottage, we can live anywhere so long as our surroundings are *charity* for our brothers and sisters.

If this is so, then rich people who visit will not feel embarrassed and the poor will not remain in the doorway....

Wherever we live, we also have to remember that our house is one where a family of true brothers and sisters live, who, because they are united in his name, have Christ among them: "For where two or three are gathered in my name, I am there among them" (Mt 18:20). This is, in fact, the phrase of the gospel that God suggested to us to throw light on this aspect of our life. If our house is the home of true brothers and sisters, united in the name of Jesus, if it is an environment that shelters a family and where each brother or sister is another Christ, we can say that the house which shelters us is *the House*. This house, sheltering true brothers and sisters in the supernatural sense, brothers and sisters who have become so as a consequence of the Christian revolution in action, welcomes a cell of the Mystical Body of Christ. The reality of brothers and sisters united in the name of Jesus is something so harmonious that it can't help but be reflected in the house which surrounds them. This harmonious reflection of unity is the characteristic of our homes....

Naturally, if the characteristic of our houses is the harmonious reflection of the life of unity of those who live there, it won't matter so much whether we have many objects or only a few to put in it, but what does matter is that these things are arranged in such a way as to be acceptable to everyone's taste and thus to contribute towards making our homes a reflection of the work of God.

And, since we should always be guided by charity, our house needs to be welcoming and, given that we must make ourselves one with the times in which we live, it should be modern.

1964[70]

Wisdom and study (indigo)

Love gives rise to wisdom. To all that has to do with this effect of love, from study to contemplation, we call *indigo*.

February 27, 1981[*]

Studying has no value for us unless it is a fruit of our love. ... If that is so, why do we want to study? Why do we never want to stop studying?

Because we love God and when you love someone, when you fall in love, you want to know all you can about the other person. We want to know all we can about God so that we love him more and more. In this way, books will not be a burden

---

[*] From a speech during a congress of Catholic bishops gathered to examine in depth the life and doctrine of the spirituality of unity.

for our soul, or something that stifles the spirit of prayer, but books will be like fuel added to the fire that will grow even bigger.

Grottaferrata,
June 12, 1960[*]

Love, if it burns within our hearts, also gives us a superior intelligence, a new light.

In this regard, I would like to tell you something very personal.

When I was still a young girl, I went to a theologian and, since he knew deeply the things of God, I asked him to speak to me about God. He answered: "My daughter, it is true that I have studied a lot. But, I would not know how to speak to you about God."

I was disappointed, but I thought that someone else could answer my question.

Later on, when the time came for me to go on to higher studies, I tried to enroll in a Catholic university, precisely with this same hope. But I wasn't admitted.

And so, I remember being filled with great anguish, desperate to find someone who would talk to me about God.

While I wept, however, a thought came to me and gave me a special sense of peace. It was like

---

[*] From a speech to young women who wish to consecrate their lives to bring unity to the world.

God within my soul saying: "Be at peace, Chiara, be at peace, I will teach you who I am!" And that's really what happened.

In fact, what is this Ideal if not a revelation, a manifestation of God, through which this light is now reaching a great number of people, including adults and children, students, Catholics and non-Catholics?

What is this Ideal? It is Wisdom, it is a superior light, it is something that invades the heart and the mind, say our bishops. Our superiors say it is a charism, a gift from God. But who taught me about God? God himself. And why does God do that? Because He knows how to teach us about himself: He is Love, love is light, and He knows how to do these things.

The Wisdom that must abide in all of us, even the youngest among us, the wisdom that goes well beyond knowledge (human knowledge is something rather paltry compared to divine Wisdom) is another aspect of our life of love. The love that produces Wisdom within us is what we call the *indigo*.

Rocca di Papa,
June 25, 1968[71]

Unity and the means of communication (violet)

In order to bring unity, which means to evangelize the world, what is absolutely necessary, the instrument that cannot be overlooked is the human person, men and women, the apostles. It's indispensable for them to be leaven, salt and light in the world. Only in this way can the means of communication bring everywhere a living faith, an ardent love, the Kingdom of God among all people. ...

But it is not only because of the goal of the Movement that we have [the means of communication] so much a part of our life.

The very *spirit* of the Movement calls for the means of communication. And this is because in the Movement we live a spirituality that is not only personal but also communitarian, collective.

This means that here, in the Movement, it is not possible to go to God alone. It means that it is not possible to grow in union with God only as individuals, but rather it has to be done together, with others. And this requires communication. And when there is need for communion among many people, it requires some means of communication, all the means of communication.

Bangkok, January 5, 1997[72]

In these times, even independently from us, humanity itself is considering itself as a unit, as one body. ...

Whatever a brother or sister who is far away from us does, [we should] feel as being done by [us] ourselves. When my eyes see, it is I who see; when my hand picks something up, it is I who pick it up; when my mind meditates on some thought, it is I who meditate. And this holds true because the parts of my body form a unity through my soul which keeps it alive. ...

The Movement is a body, a presence of Christ who has all the basic qualities required by the gospel.

From the diary,
August 18, 1970

This modest magazine [Città Nuova] seeks to help people who are sensitive to unity and desire it, to fulfill this ideal, which Jesus asked for 2,000 years ago in his Testament. ...

It aims to be a publication for everyone, to which everyone can contribute, whether they are gifted in writing or not, unknown or famous, religious or lay, laborers or professionals, men or women. ...

It does not seek to be ostentatious, or include only the most popular journalists ... What is of interest is the truth, stated out of love for the common good, and for each individual. ...

Our magazine aims at being a meeting point for those who want to bear witness to Christ in the fullest possible unity.

March 1957[73]

The fable that blossomed along Foco Lane

We conclude the chapter on the "aspects/ colors" with this text, which is a parable about the life of unity, with its beauty, its demands, its nearly irresistible attraction. Because it is unity in variety, it composes a harmony which is the Kingdom of God on earth.

On the windowsill of a small mountain cottage were many little pots of flowers.

Red, white, pink and blue.

During the night, Someone passed by and cast into one pot a small seed.

The next day, upon the death of the tiny flower that was occupying the pot, people passing by saw there a magnificent flower never seen before, gleaming - a little star.

In the flowerpots next to this one, little by little, the humble tiny mountain flowers died and upon their death blossomed many stars.

They were like the first star and yet different: one, though shining brightly, was tinted red, another blue, another yellow, and another violet, and so forth.

Little by little, from all sides surrounding the cottage, other flowerpots fled from their windowsills and gardens to take their place beside the little flowerpots of stars, eager for death and for light.

They also came from afar: from large cities, rich with precious flowers, like roses, carnations and lilies.

As soon as they settled down next to the first flowerpots, some on other windowsills, some on the lawn that ran along the small wall, some on the roof and others on the chimney ... they died without complaint.

And like a miracle, in all of them, stars blossomed forth: little stars which were more red than luminous, more blue than resplendent ... more colorful than bright.

And next to the little shining star that had a red hue, all the other red-colored flowers drew close, and so with the others.

One day, beside the first star, in the same pot, a tiny shoot emerged.

It seemed separate from the first plant, but beneath the soil it was linked to it. On it blossomed a little star, smaller than the first star but of the same brilliance.

All the stars loved one another, praised each other's beauty and were not envious of what was beautiful in the others.

It was for this reason that another day, a flowerpot with a very rare and delicate flower was able to place itself beside the first flowerpot.

The flower died and in its place there appeared, not a star, but a small fire.

It was night. Someone flew over that enchanted place. He saw the firmament on earth, heard the gentle rustling of countless small flowerpots rushing toward the starry cottage and said:

"Sicut in coelo et in terra" [On earth as it is in heaven].

From a written passage, Summer 1950

Conclusion

We close this collection with some passages from the Diary that express Chiara's "gratitude" for the gift of unity revealed in John 17.

Chiara comments on the first verse of John 17: "He looked up to heaven and said, 'Father, the hour has come; glorify your Son so that the Son may glorify you."

It is magnificent this divine mutual help between Son and Father to advance their cause, which is that of Truth, of Love, of Freedom, of All.

And although he prays with human words, you sense he is God, a person of the Trinity. The plan of salvation is reaching its climax. Unity is about to be unleased between heaven and earth; the reconciliation of humankind with God is about to begin.

What a great hour! It is solemn, so solemn. This prayer could only be pronounced out loud—anything that is solemn is open, glorious, powerful! The words that follow express the truth that the glory which the Son gives to the Father will be accomplished: "Since you have given him authority over all people, to give eternal life to all whom you have given him."

Little by little, as Christ is announced to the world, and with him the Father, the glory grows. "And this is eternal life, that they may know you, the only true God, and Jesus Christ whom you have sent."

From the Diary, June 29, 1970

A heart full of human-divine love

Chiara comments John 17:13: "But now I am coming to you, and I speak these things in the world so that they may have my joy made complete in themselves."

What loving insistence, what abundance, what wealth of personal affection, so true, so alive in your heart, Jesus, for your people!

Oh! that heart, that heart! We will never talk enough about your heart which, just as two thousand years ago, is still now in heaven. That heart made you do crazy things. You no longer knew what reasons to put forward to obtain the benevolent gaze of the Father on your people....

In this passage it seems, moreover, that you realize that others are listening to you, and hearing will be comforted by this all-powerful prayer 'll experience, from that very moment, their 'ng up, as they participate in your communion with the Father, where there is the fullness of joy.

From the diary, July 13, 1970

The "I desire" of love

Chiara comments on John 17:24: "Father, I desire that those also, whom you have given me, may be with me where I am, to see my glory, which you have given me because you loved me before the foundation of the world."

Perhaps this is the part of the testament that most astonished me the very first time I read it.

Never, never on earth has such a thing been heard. . . .

I desire: it's the *desire* of love. The *desire* that has a little echo in the "desire" of the saints, such as in the letters of Catherine [of Siena]. The *desire* of one who is "extra-convinced" of asking only for things that are pleasing to the one who is being asked and to those for whom one is praying, and of someone who is convinced of asking for *great* things.

He wants us to *see* his glory. He's going into his kingdom and wants to take us with him.

He has a treasure to show to his friends and love leads him to keep nothing hidden from them; rather there is such passion in his prayer that it gives the impression he is willing to do anything so that we might savor who he is and participate in his life. He is speaking of a reality, the reality of God, which existed before the foundation of the world. ...

If our heart does not burn for love of him, if our life does not cut with all that is not him or for him, we are less than human, we are irresponsible and ungrateful.

From the diary, July 22, 1970

Endnotes

1   General Audience, September 25, 2013.

2   Chiara Lubich, *A New Way,* (New York: New City Press, 2006), 54.

3   Ignace de la Potterie, *La vérité dans Saint Jean,* II, Rome: P.I.B., 1977,.724; cited in Gerard Rossé, *L'ultima preghiera di Gesù* (Rome: Città Nuova, 1988), 103.

4   "Le desir d'un auteur est que son oeuvre s'acheve dans une ame," in Jean Guitton, *Le travail intellectuel* (Paris: Aubier, 1951, 1986), 99.

5   From a written passage in *Jesus, The Heart of His Message: Unity and Jesus Forsaken,* Chiara Lubich, (New York: New City Press, 1985), 23.

6   From the article "The Testament of Jesus," written for the magazine *Città Nuova,* 3 (1959) 23: 3.

7   From a speech to lay people committed to live unity in all aspects of social and political life. Unpublished in its original version, reproduced here. See also Chiara Lubich, *A Call To* Love (New York: New City Press, 1990), 108.

8   From *Fides* (October, 1948):, 279–280, "Unity and Community—The Christian Community." See also Chiara Lubich and Igino Giordani, *Erano i tempi di Guerra* (Rome: Città Nuova, 2007), 44–48.

9   See Igino Giordani, *Diary of Fire* (New York: New City Press, 1981), 38.

10 *Un po' di storia del "Movimento dell'Unità"* (Trent: Tipografia AOR, 1950), 12. See also *Nuova Umanità* 31 (2009/1) 181: 23–24; 27–28.

11 From a letter to Anna Melchiori, as cited in Chiara Lubich, *Early Letters* (New York: New City Press, 2014), 58. Edited. In *Early Letters* it is dated 1945.

12 From a letter to Father Bonaventure da Malé, O.F.M. Cap. as cited in Chiara Lubich, *Early Letters* (New York: New City Press, 2014), 90–91. Edited.

13 From a letter to Father Valeriani, O.F.M. Conv. as cited in Chiara Lubich, *Early Letters* (New York: New City Press, 2014), 99. Edited.

14 From a written passage cited in Chiara Lubich, *Essential Writings* (New York: New City Press, 2007), 98.

15 From a speech to directors of the Focolare Movement from around the world. Unpublished in its original version, reproduced here. See *Jesus, The Heart of His Message* (New York: New City Press, 1985), 22.

16 From a telephone conference call as cited in Chiara Lubich, *Cercando le cose di lassù* (Rome: Città Nuova, 1992), 155–156.

17 From a letter to Father Massimei, O.F.M. Conv. cited in *Essential Writings*, 318.

18 From a letter to a group of consecrated religious cited in *Essential Writings*, 108.

19 From a letter to Father Raffaele Massimei, O.F.M. Conv., cited in *Early Letters*, 111–112. Edited.

20 From a letter addressed to Father Bonaventura and other consecrated religious men, cited in *Early Letters*, 135–136. Edited.

21 ORIGEN, *Comm. In Matth.* XIV, 1s: PG 13, 1187

22 From a telephone conference call cited in Chiara Lubich, *Santità di popolo* (Rome: Città Nuova, 2001), 95–96.

23 From the passage "Unity" in *Nuova Umanità* 29 (2007/6) 174: 605–606.

24 From a telephone conference call cited in Chiara Lubich, *Santi insieme* (Rome: Città Nuova, 1995), 82–83.

25 From a letter to Sister Josefina and Sister Fidente cited in *Early Letters*, 65.

26 From a speech to a group of consecrated religious men of various orders and congregations bound together by the spirituality of unity. A published version of the talk can be found in *Pregare come angeli*, Natalia Dallapiccola and Enzo Maria Fondi, eds., 17. For internal use of the Focolare Movement.

27 From the article, "Solitude and Unity" in *Città Nuova* 11 (1975), 33.

28 From a talk to Focolare directors from around the world. Unpublished in its original version, reproduced here. See *The Eucharist* (New York: New City Press, 2005), 57–58.

29 From a comment on the Word of life: "I am the vine, you are the branches. Those who abide in me and I in them bear much fruit, because apart from me you can do nothing." (Jn 15:5) cited in *Essential Writings*, 76.

30 See Chiara Lubich, *The Cry of Jesus Crucified and Forsaken* (New York: New City Press, 2001), 60.

31 See "Paradise '49," *Claritas: Journal of Dialogue and Culture*: Vol. 1: No. 1, Article 3, http://docs.lib.purdue. edu/claritas/vol1/iss1/3.

32 See *The Cry*, 61.

33 See Chiara Lubich, *Mary, The Transparency of God*, (New York: New City Press, 2001), 29.

34 *Il patto del '49 nell'esperienza di Chiara Lubich: Percorsi interdisciplinari*, (Rome: Città Nuova, 2012) p. 20.

35 Ibid., 7.

36 From a written passage in "Paradise '49," *Claritas, A Journal of Dialogue and Culture*, 1 (March 2012): 7–8. http://docs.lib.purdue.edu/claritas/vol1/iss1/3.

37 *Essential Writings*, 36–37

38 From a telephone conference call in *Santità di popolo*, 70.

39 From a letter to consecrated religious men of Assisi cited in *Early Letters*, 98. Edited.

40 From a telephone conference call cited in Chiara Lubich, *La vita un viaggio* (Rome: Città Nuova, Roma 1994), 32–33.

41 Unpublished document.

42 *Early Letters*, 58.

43 From a written passage cited in *L'Unità*, *Nuova Umanità* 29 (2007/6) 174: 607.

44 From a written passage cited in *L'Unità*, *Nuova Umanità* 29 (2007/6) 174: 610.

45 *Essential Writings*, 100–101.

46 From a written passage in *Nuova Umanità* 29 (2007/6) 174: 609.

47 From the published version of the diary found in *Cristo dispiegato nei secoli: Testi scelti* (Rome: Città Nuova, 1994), 118–119.

48 From the answers during a festival organized by youth of the Focolare Movement for their peers. A published version of this answer can be found in *Cercate la pienezza della gioia. 50 risposte ai giovani* (Rome: Città Nuova, 2012), 7.

49 "The Church is charity, the Church is unity," address of Paul VI to the participants in the Pan Oceanic Episcopal Conference, December 2, 1970.

50 See Message of John Paul II to the spiritual congress of bishops, friends of the Focolare Movement, February 14, 2001.

51 From a letter to Father Massimei cited in *Early Letters*, 102. Edited.

52 From a letter addressed to four consecrated men religious who lived in the international College on Via Sicilia, Rome, and had come to know the Ideal of unity, cited in *Early Letters*, 137–38. Edited.

53 From a telephone conference call in *Santi insieme*, 54.

54 From a speech in St. Peter's, the Reformed Cathedral of Geneva. See published version in *Living Dialogue* (New York: New City Press, 2009), 42–44.

55 From a speech to the World Council of Churches. See published version in *Living Dialogue*, 59–61.

56 Prayer for unity offered in the chapel of the World Council of Churches. See published version in Living Dialogue, 45–47.

57 From a speech to the International Conference "A Culture of Peace for the Unity of Peoples," promoted by the Focolare Movement as cited in *Per una civiltà dell'unità*, in Atti del convegno "Una cultura di pace per l'unità dei popoli," Castel Gandolfo (Rome), June 11–12, 1988: 10–18.

58 From a speech to directors of the Focolare Movement from around the world cited in *A New* Way, 169–70

59 From a speech during a conference of bishops of the Catholic Church who wish to examine in depth the life and doctrine of the spirituality of unity. The published version of the speech can be found in *A New Way*, 75–77.

60 From a written passage. Inserted as the premise to the volume *Come un arcobaleno* (Rome: 2000). For private circulation in the Focolare Movement.

61 From a speech to Focolare Movement directors around the world cited in *A New Way*, 50.

62 From a speech to members who are consecrated in the Focolare in order to spread the spirit of unity. A published version of the speech can be found in *La carità come ideale* (Rome: Città Nuova, 1971), 43–44.

63 From a speech to members who are consecrated in the Focolare in order to spread the spirit of unity cited in *A New Way*, 79–80.

64 From a speech to members who are consecrated to God in the Focolare to spread the spirit of unity. Unpublished speech of December 25, 1962, reprised by Chiara Lubich in a talk to the focolarine on December 28, 1997. A published version can be found in *A New Way*, 90–91.

65   From a dialogue with a large group of people gathered to examine in depth the spirituality of unity. This answer can be found in the edited version of the publication *Come un arcobaleno*, 261–262.

66   From a speech on the seven colors of the rainbow to a group of people gathered in a congress called "Mariapolis, City of Mary" found in the edited version of the publication *Come un arcobaleno*, 281.

67   From a speech to youth committed to witnessing and spreading the spirituality of unity. A published version of the speech can be found in *Colloqui con i Gen anni 1966/69* (Rome: Città Nuova, 1998), 69.

68   *Meditazioni* (Rome: Città Nuova, [1959] 2008), 36–37. Also in *Essential Writings*, 99.

69   From an address during the conferral of an honorary doctorate in Psychology, Malta as cited in *Essential Writings*, 228–29.

70   From a speech on the seven colors of the rainbow to a group of people gathered in a congress called "Mariapolis, City of Mary" cited in *Come un arcobaleno*, 439–441.

71   From a dialogue with young persons committed to the witness and spreading of the spirit of unity cited in *Colloqui con i Gen anni 1966/6* (Rome: Città Nuova, 1998), 69.

72   From an address during the conferment of an honorary doctorate in Social Communications, Bangkok cited in *Nuova Umanità* XIX [1997/2], 110: 204.

73   From the article "This Page" from the magazine "Città Nuova," [New City] which for some months was called "La Rete" [The Network]. *La rete*, 1 (March, 1957).

About Chiara Lubich

Chiara Lubich (1920-2008) was founder of the Focolare Movement (The Work of Mary). Born in Trent, Italy, her baptismal name was Silvia. In 1943, when she entered the Third Franciscan Order, she took the name Chiara because she was attracted by St. Clare of Assisi's radical choice of God. 1943 also marks the year that Chiara Lubich made a vow of chastity, and it has become the year associated with the birth of the Focolare. In the course of her life, she saw the spirituality of the Focolare – the spirituality of unity – grow around the world. She was awarded 15 honorary doctoral degrees, numerous civic awards, the Templeton Prize for Progress of Religion, and the UNESCO Peace Prize. She has published more than 50 books in 29 languages.

Today, the Focolare Movement that she founded is present in 182 countries. It has approximately 2 million adherents and people who are sympathetic to its goals – the majority being Roman Catholic. There is a growing number of non-Catholics from 350 churches and ecclesial communities. The Movement also includes many from other world faiths for example Jews, Muslims, Buddhists, Hindus and Sikhs. Then there are also those in the Movement who do not adhere to any particular religious faith.

The following titles are based on the thought and experience of Chiara Lubich.

Biography

Eran Tiempos De Guerra,* 2009, 950-586-235-1, $23.95
La Mirada De Chiara Lubich, 2008, 950-586-232-6, $21.50
May They All Be One (E-book), 1972, 71-77438,
                                          Coming Soon
Stars and Tears (NCL),† 1990, 0-904287-25-4, $14.99

Economy and Work

Economia De Comunion, Historia, 2003, 950-586-174-5,
                                              $11.95

Ecumenical and Interreligious Dialogue

Living Dialogue, 2009, 978-1-56548-326-2, $9.95
Living Dialogue (E-book), 2009, $9.95

Family Life

Donde Florece La Vida, 2009, 950-586-121-4, $18.95
Love That Comes from God, 1995, 978-1-56548-030-8,
                                              $9.95
Love That Comes from God (E-book), 1995,   Coming Soon

God is Love

God Loves You Immensely, 2010, 978-1-56548-339-2,
                                              $6.95
God Loves You Immensely (E-book), 2010, $6.95

Jesus Forsaken

¿Por Que Me Has Abandonado?, 2008, 950-586-130-3,
                                              $17.50
Cry of Jesus Crucified and Forsaken, 2001,
                978-1-56548-159-6, $11.95
Jesus: The Heart of His Message, 1985,
                978-1-56548-090-2, $8.95
Jesus: The Heart of His Message Ebook, 1985,
                978-1-56548-090-2,   Coming Soon

---

*   Spanish Titles are in *Blue*
†   NCL indicates published by New City London

Only at Night We See the Stars, 2002, 978-1-56548-158-9,
$11.95
The Choice of Jesus Forsaken, 2015, 978-1-56548-580-8,
Coming Soon

Jesus in the Midst

United In His Name, 1992, 978-1-56548-003-2, $11.95
United In His Name (Ebook), 1992, 978-1-56548-003-2,
Coming Soon

Love of Neighbor

The Art of Loving, 2010, 978-1-56548-335-4, $11.95
El Amor Al Hermano, 2012, 950-586-296-2, $19.95
El Arte De Amar, 2004, 950-586-203-2, $18.95
Neighbors, 2012, 978-1-56548-476-4, $6.95
Neighbors (E-book), 2012, 978-1-56548-466-5, $4.95

Mary

Maria, Transparencia De Dios, 2003, 950-586-172-9, $13.50
Mary—The Transparency of God, 2003, 978-1-56548-192-3,
$11.95
Mary—The Transparency of God (Ebook), 2003,
978-1-56548-192-3, $9.99

Meditations

Fragments of Wisdom/Stirrings of Unity (Ebook),
1964, 64-24944,   Coming Soon
Fragments of Wisdom/Stirrings of Unity (NCL), 1964,
64-24944, $12.99
Heaven on Earth, 2000, 978-1-56548-144-2, $12.95
It's a whole new scene (Ebook), 1970, 78-133629, c
Coming Soon
Knowing How to Lose (Ebook), 1981, 0-904287-16-5,
Coming Soon
Knowing How to Lose (NCL), 1981, 0-904287-16-5, $12.99
Little harmless manifesto (Ebook), 1973, 72-97595,
Coming Soon
Meditaciones, 2013, 978-950-586-150-8, $13.50

Meditations (Ebook), 1990, 978-0-904287-93-6,
Coming Soon
Meditations - hard cover (NCL), 1990, 978-0-904287-93-6,
$14.99
No Thorn Without a Rose (99, cloth.), 2008,
978-1-56548-294-4, $14.95
No Thorn Without a Rose (99, paper.), 2008,
978-1-56548-295-1, $9.95
No Thorn without a Rose (Ebook), 2008, 978-1-56548-420-7,
$9.95
Yes Yes No No (Ebook), 1977, 0-904287-07-6, Coming Soon
Yes Yes No No (NCL), 1977, 0-904287-07-6, $12.99

Mutual Love

El Amor Reciproco, 2013, 978-950-586-305-1, $19.95
The Pearl, 2013, 978-1-56548-495-5, $6.95
The Pearl (Ebook), 2013, 978-1-56548-541-9, $6.95
When Our Love Is Charity—Spiritual Writings Vol. 2,
1991, 978-0-911782-93-6, $9.95

Spirituality of Unity

Journey to Heaven, 1997, 978-1-56548-093-3, $8.95
Journey to Heaven (Ebook), 1997, 978-1-56548-093-3,
Coming Soon

The Church

Servants of All (NCL), 1990, 0-911782-05-2, $12.99

The Eucharist

Eucharist, 2005, 978-1-56548-224-1, $7.95
Eucharist (Ebook), 2014, 978-1-56548-224-1, $2.95
Jesus Eucharistia, 2014, 978-950-586-317-4 18.95
The Sun that Daily Rises, 2014, 978-1-56548-552-5, $6.95
The Sun that Daily Rises (audio), 2014, 978-1-56548-552-5,
$2.99
The Sun that Daily Rises (Ebook), 2014, 978-1-56548-552-5,
$2.95

The Present Moment

Here and Now (revised ed.), 2005, 978-1-56548-232-6, $7.95

The Will of God

Man's Yes to God (NCL), 1990, 0-911782-38-9,	$12.99
Rays, 2010, 978-1-56548-382-8,	$6.95
Rays (Ebook), 2010, 978-1-56548-385-9,	$4.95

The Word of God

God's Word to Us, 2011, 978-1-56548-425-2,	$6.95
God's Word to Us (Ebook), 2011, 978-1-56548-442-9,	$4.95

Unity

Unity, 2015, 978-1-56548-593-8,	$14.95

Writings

A New Way, 2006, 978-1-56548-236-4,	$12.95
Diary 1964/65, 1987, 0-911782-55-9,	$12.99
Early Letters, 2012, 978-1-56548-432-0,	$15.95
Early Letters (Ebook), 2012, 978-1-56548-464-1,	$9.99
Essential Writings: Chiara Lubich, 2007, 978-1-56548-259-3,	$24.95
Essential Writings (Ebook), 2009, 978-1-56548-347-7,	$9.95
On the Holy Journey, 1988, 0-911782-60-5,	$12.99
The Living Presence (NCL), 1990, 978-0-904287-55-4,	$12.99
Un Camino Nuevo, 2010, 978-950-586-170-5,	$18.95

New City Press
of the Focolare
Hyde Park, New York

New City Press is one of more than 20 publishing houses sponsored by the Focolare, a movement founded by Chiara Lubich to help bring about the realization of Jesus' prayer: "That all may be one" (John 17:21). In view of that goal, New City Press publishes books and resources that enrich the lives of people and help all to strive toward the unity of the entire human family. We are a member of the Association of Catholic Publishers.

www.NewCityPress.com

Scan to join our mailing list for discounts and promotions

Periodicals
Living City Magazine, www.livingcitymagazine.com